The Nursery Year in Action

Child-led learning in the early years allows children to thrive while making accelerated progress. Young children learn and develop best when they are in a stimulating environment that is carefully organised and equipped to meet their needs, interests and stages of development, and where each child's progress is carefully observed, managed and enhanced by adults who engage and interact with them to support them in making outstanding progress.

Demonstrating how a child-led approach supports the development of purposeful, calm, confident and independent children, *The Nursery Year in Action* offers a unique month-by-month overview of the workings of an outstanding nursery setting. The book covers all aspects of practice from the organisation of the classroom and garden and the rationale behind this to the routines and boundaries that ensure children are safe, happy and therefore able to explore and learn. It tracks the events of each month in the year paying particular attention to the environment, the role of the adult, links with parents, children's individual needs and the key areas of learning and development. Throughout the book Anna Ephgrave gives the reason behind each decision and shows what the outcomes have been for the children, emphasising that a child-led approach, with planning in the moment can meet the requirements of the revised Early Years Foundation Stage and the individual needs of the children.

Key features include:

- over 150 full colour photographs to illustrate practice;
- photocopiable pages of planning and record-keeping sheets;
- lists of resources and materials;
- examples of 'individual learning journeys' and 'planning in the moment' for groups;
- guidance on what to look for when assessing children's progress;
- advice on benefit/risk assessments;
- suggestions for managing transitions and minimising stress.

Written by a leading consultant teacher whose early years' department has achieved 'Outstanding' at four consecutive OFSTED inspections, this book provides practitioners with the practical ideas to work with confidence in a way that is rewarding, manageable and, above all, creates a happy, relaxed learning environment for children.

Anna Ephgrave is Assistant Head Teacher responsible for the Early Years at Carterhatch Infant School and Children's Centres. Her first book *The Reception Year in Action* has inspired and supported settings both in the UK and abroad. She now works part time as a consultant, both nationally and internationally.

The Nursery Year in Action

Following children's interests through the year

Anna Ephgrave

 Routledge
Taylor & Francis Group

LONDON AND NEW YORK

First published 2015
by Routledge
2 Park Square, Milton Park, Abingdon, Oxon OX14 4RN

and by Routledge
711 Third Avenue, New York, NY 10017

Routledge is an imprint of the Taylor & Francis Group, an informa business

British Library Cataloguing in Publication Data
A catalogue record for this book is available from the British Library

Library of Congress Cataloging in Publication Data
Ephgrave, Anna.
The nursery year in action : following children's interests through the year / Anna Ephgrave.
pages cm
Includes bibliographical references and index.
1. Education, Preschool—Activity programs. 2. Education—Parent participation. 3. Student participation in curriculum planning. 4. Home and school. I. Title.
LB1140.2.E74 2015
372.21—dc23
2014042662

ISBN: 978-1-138-88522-6 (hbk)
ISBN: 978-0-415-82004-2 (pbk)
ISBN: 978-1-315-71559-9 (ebk)

Typeset in Bembo
by FiSH Books Ltd, Enfield

Contents

List of figures

Foreword

It gives me enormous pleasure to write this foreword for *The Nursery Year in Action*. I met Anna Ephgrave five years ago in action in her class. I was bowled over and could hardly contain myself in wanting to express my gratitude to Ruth for telling me to go and visit her! And to tell everyone about Anna's practice. Everything I believed in was happening in her class and garden.

I think what impressed me the most was the independence of the children. Children were absorbed in what they were doing but aware that their activities could take any turn as the staff and environment would facilitate and support them. Staff talked and listened to children and were quite clearly enjoying their work. The conversations were about real things, involving sympathetic questioning to help children achieve their plans and ideas. Inside and out were one, the two spaces just merged. If a child needed something from inside they went and got it and if they needed something outside they did likewise. Children were not arguing and squabbling, they were getting on with the joy of learning. There was a palpable sense of excitement and eager anticipation throughout the day and I left having learnt a great deal and so did every single child, eager to return tomorrow.

It was therefore fantastic news when *The Reception Year in Action* came out, so all could experience and learn from Anna's practice and success. I have met so many teachers and students who have found Anna's book invaluable. *The Nursery Year in Action* is equally fantastic and covers a year in the life of early years classes in one infant school. Each chapter covers one month and includes sections about the organisation and the environment, and a diary of events. Everything one needs to know about early years practice is included. Anna demonstrates that one does not need forward planning, or focused activities, but that one must be absolutely clear about one's philosophy of education, crystal clear about how to achieve one's ambitions for children and fully able to justify and defend one's practice. At the heart of all that Anna does is children's development and learning, and under Anna's guidance children learn and develop dramatically.

Good early years practice changes lives. It is highly effective in helping children learn and develop emotionally, socially, physically, cognitively and linguistically. But it isn't easy to do well and it takes effort to fully understand. This book makes understanding that unique early years approach easy. Anna's style of writing is open and accessible. Everyone who is involved with early years education and care should read this book.

Helen Bilton
National Teaching Fellow and Associate Professor in Education, University of Reading

Acknowledgements

This book is based on one year in Carterhatch Infant School nursery class. Although my name is on the cover, there are so many other people who have made the book possible and I would like to thank them. First, I must thank Andrew Boyes, the head teacher, who appointed me as Assistant Head Teacher for early years at Carterhatch. He has given me support and encouragement to work in the school and to lead the early years following a truly child-led pedagogy. Without his backing, this book would not have been possible.

The biggest thanks must go to Jacqui Granger, the nursery class teacher. She is a highly skilled practitioner, who has worked with such energy, determination and enthusiasm to make the nursery outstanding. In addition she met with me on numerous occasions to share hundreds of photos and stories from the class. Without her meticulous organisation and superb memory, the book would not be as vibrant and honest as it is. Jacqui also had support from many other practitioners and I thank them too: Rachel, Pem, Melissa, Loretta, Sam and Charlene.

Of course, a very special thanks must go to the children – thank you for being so fascinating, inquisitive, exciting, happy, thoughtful, challenging, energetic, funny, creative, lively – in other words, thank you for being children. Finally, thank you to the parents who have allowed their children to be included in this project, resulting in a book that I hope will be enjoyed by many.

Introduction

Pedagogy

If you visited the nursery class at Carterhatch Infant School, you would see 45 children who are purposeful, calm, confident and independent. You would see adults moving to where the children are engaged and interacting with them as they play. You would see a superb environment that is equipped to meet the needs, interests and stages of development of each child. You would see children who are making outstanding progress.

You would *not* see any forward planning, nor would you see any focus activities and you would not see adults telling children which activity to do.

To work in this way involves complex arrangements and yet the reasoning is simple. After more than 25 years teaching I am confident that this child-led approach to teaching in the early years (including reception) **is best for the children**.

In summary this is my pedagogy:

> Children are born with a natural desire to explore and learn and practitioners can support them in this. We do this by creating an enabling environment (both physical and emotional) and through the relationships and interactions that the children experience. **We do not plan ahead**, rather we remain 'in the moment' with the children as they explore and learn. We observe carefully, and enhance the learning whenever we spot a 'teachable moment'. Our observations, interactions and the outcomes are recorded afterwards.

This is a simple message – **let the children choose what to do, join them and support them in their pursuits and then write up what has happened**. The rest of this book will explain in detail how this looks in practice and what outcomes are achieved.

For anyone about to abandon this book already, let me state that I have been through **four OFSTED** (Office for Standards in Education, Children's Services and Skills) **inspections** since adopting this approach (with two under the revised EYFS (Early Years Foundation Stage) and new OFSTED framework) and on each occasion my early years department has achieved '**Outstanding**'. That is without any forward planning and without any focus activities. What is more important is that, since adopting this approach, I have seen happy, relaxed children making accelerated progress as well as staff who are relaxed, inspired and enthusiastic, having regained a love of their job. It's a 'win-win' approach and I would urge you to read on.

Brain development

Babies are born with billions of brain cells and with stimulation these cells connect and form synapses. This is brain development, this is a child making 'progress', this is when a brain is 'lit up'. Without stimulation the brain will not develop fully. This has been illustrated all too starkly in the case of the children from the Romanian orphanages. These children were fed and clean but they were left in cots without interaction or stimulation, for up to three years of their lives. Their brain scans show gaps in their brains, particularly in the temporal lobes – areas that regulate emotions and receive input from the senses. These children struggle to develop empathy and have cognitive delays.

It is vital, therefore, that young children are stimulated and that the opportunities for synapse development are maximised. We need their brains to be 'lit up' as much as possible. Brain activity and synapse formation are at their highest when a child is deeply engrossed in something that fascinates, challenges and makes them happy. Every child is unique and we cannot predict or impose what will spark that deep fascination. Each child is at a different level of development and therefore something that will challenge one child will be mundane for the next. Equally one child will be at their happiest digging in the mud while another will enjoy sitting and drawing a wonderful picture. We need to organise the setting so that each child can excel in his or her own unique way. We do not need brain scanners to know when their brains are developing or 'lit up'. We can use a very simple measure: the **Levels of Involvement Scale** developed by Professor Ferre Laevers.

Levels of involvement

The scale has five levels (see Appendix A). Level 5 is high-level involvement and is characterised by the child showing continuous and intense activity with concentration, creativity, energy and persistence. Deep-level learning, with many parts of the brain 'lit up', is known to occur when children operate at this level of involvement.

In contrast, low-level involvement (Level 1) is characterised by activity that is simple, stereotypic, repetitive and passive, with little or no challenge and with the child appearing absent and displaying no energy. When children are operating at this level, there is very little brain activity and minimal learning.

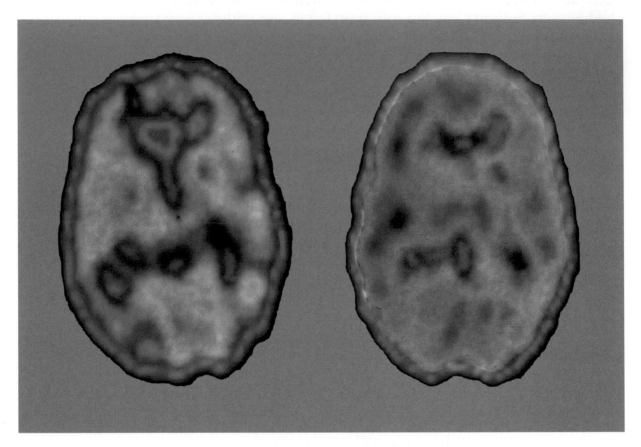

Passive/Sad – level 1
Low level involvement
Minimal learning

Purposeful/Happy – level 5
High level involvement
Deep level learning

These 5 levels of involvement can be used to assess individuals, groups or a whole class. Ferre Laevers also has a scale for the assessment of 'emotional well-being' but experience has shown that the two scales are very closely connected. For example, a child who is consistently displaying low-level involvement, in spite of an outstanding environment and excellent practitioners, is very likely to have some emotional problem – perhaps related to an issue at home. However, the assessment of the level of involvement is the first step in assessing an individual or a setting.

Anyone who visits our nursery (or reception classes) comments on how calm and purposeful the children are. They are actually assessing the levels of involvement, the amount of brain activity and the amount of progress that is happening. They can see that the children are not stressed and nor are the staff. (Stress causes areas of the brain to shut down and therefore development is hindered.) The children are displaying high levels of involvement and so are the staff. I will endeavour, through this book, to explain how this can be achieved.

Organisation of the book

There are 11 chapters in the book – one for each month of the year that the school is open. Most chapters are divided into three sections. The first section looks at general, organisational, practical or theoretical issues – such as data, adult roles, toilet training, induction and budgets. These may be related to the particular month in which they appear or they may be on-going issues; the second section is devoted to the description of various aspects of the physical environment. In order to meet the needs, stage of development and interests of each child, the provision and resources are crucially important. This is why a large proportion of the book is devoted to this subject. The third section is a diary of the events from that particular month – illustrating the teaching and learning that is happening constantly. This includes the interactions between the staff and the children and between groups of children as well as examples of the independent learning that occur.

Any early years setting is a highly complicated organisation and everything has to be in place to achieve an outstanding outcome. I would like to give all the information at once. Each piece of information forms part of the whole picture and although you can dip in and out of each chapter, I hope you will read the whole book to ensure that you understand the complete rationale.

Carterhatch Infant School and children's centres

My role at Carterhatch is Assistant Head Teacher for Early Years. I manage the nursery and reception classes. There are three reception classes with 30 children in each and they are run in exactly the same way as the nursery (except for ten minute phonic sessions each day in reception). The school has two children's centres attached to it, one of which is on the same site as the school. The 3–5's provision for this children's centre is based in the same room as the school nursery and caters for 16 children at any one time, with two members of staff. The school nursery class has 60 children on role (30 morning and 30 afternoon) with a teacher, Jacqui Granger, and three support staff. Therefore, at any one time, there are 46 children and six staff in the nursery room and garden. All rooms at the children's centres are organised in line with the messages in this book – no forward planning, an outstanding environment, responsive adults who work 'in the moment' with the babies and young children, and written accounts of the teaching and learning that occur.

Current legislation

As I write this book, we are working under the revised EYFS and a new OFSTED Framework. Everything described in this book meets the current legal requirements – the recent OFSTED inspections confirm this. However, more important is the fact that we are delivering **excellent early years practice that is best for the children**. Going forward, we will continue to do what is best for young children, even if it conflicts with government decisions. As practitioners, we need to be passionate and determined in our defence of best early years practice. The 'top down' pressure for the 'schoolification' of the early years is intense. We need to demonstrate that children can achieve outstanding progress by playing, following their hearts, pursuing their interests and taking risks. The environment and interactions that we offer are crucial in this endeavour. I hope this book will help practitioners feel confident and inspired to trust that children have a natural desire to explore and learn. The book should also give ideas on how best to support children's exploration and learning through the environment and the interactions that we offer.

1 September

SEPTEMBER: TO DO LIST

- Attend staff training.
- Home visit all the children.
- Alert agencies of any concerns after home visits.
- Prepare the class environment – indoors and outside.
- Prepare a coat peg, self-register and an individual folder for each child.
- Organise groups of children to start nursery.
- Welcome and support children and their families.
- Focus on PSE to ensure children are happy and expectations of behaviour are clear.
- Start initial assessments.

Since September is such a special month, this chapter is organised differently from the remaining chapters in the book. The 'To Do List' above gives just a hint as to the vast amount of work that is done in this month. I will describe how the month is organised, explain home visits and explore the general principals of how the physical environment is organised. I will go on to explain how the children are introduced to the nursery and the role of the staff at this critical time. There is a short 'Diary' section, in which you can see how the induction work continues and the children begin to explore and learn in their new environment. Although we start initial assessments of the children in September, the bulk of this work is done in October and will be described in that chapter.

For many settings, September is a unique month and this is certainly the case for school-based nurseries. The academic year starts in September and therefore this is the month when a huge number of transitions occur – from home to pre-school, from pre-school to nursery, from nursery to reception. All over the country, children are moving to new settings. In many nursery settings the new children join children who are already established in the environment. For others, all the children are new to the setting. It is crucial that their induction ensures a smooth transition into the nursery class. This requires meticulous planning and preparation. Much of this work was started in the summer term and will be described in later chapters of this book. Here I will set out the work we do in September and how the children are inducted into the nursery.

September timetable

The usual timetable for the month of September in school is presented in Figure 1.1.

Week 1	2 days preparing class and garden 3 days home visits
Week 2	5 days home visits
Week 3	2 days home visits First groups start nursery (attending for two sessions per week)
Week 4	Remaining groups start nursery Initial assessments completed for some children

Figure 1.1 September timetable

Thus, by the end of September, all the children have been visited at home, the nursery environment is prepared and all the children are attending nursery for at least two sessions per week. Some initial assessments will also have been completed.

Home visits

In the supermarket last week I met a boy who is now in Year 4. He smiled and said 'Hello Anna. I remember when you came to my house!'. Six years on and that visit was still a vivid and positive memory for that child! It is easy to forget what a huge, life-changing experience it is for a three year old to step into nursery on that first day. The home visit is one way to ease that step by making the staff members familiar to the child and introducing them in the environment where the child is most at ease – their home. Even if the child is shy and quiet during the visit, they will be watching and listening and they

will remember your faces when they arrive at nursery for their first session. Some settings carry out home visits in July and I do worry that the gap between the visit and their first day at nursery may be too long for such young children.

We usually manage six visits per day – depending on distances to be travelled – and the teacher attends with another member of the nursery team. The visit usually lasts about 40 minutes, with one adult talking to a parent, making links with the family and filling in necessary paperwork and the other adult playing with the child. We have made an information booklet for the families and this helps to structure the conversation with

the parent and to ensure that we pass on all information necessary. The booklet is left with the family so they can refer back for information as they need it. The booklet covers the curriculum, how the nursery is run, staffing, term dates, clothing, contact numbers etc. It has lots of colour photos to make it attractive to the children and also to help with comprehension for parents who have little English.

In terms of information we gain from the family, we have a form to fill in (see Figure 1.2). However, if at all possible we hope that a frank and open conversation develops and the family can relax. In this way, we gain truly valuable information about the child and family and begin to develop a partnership. We try to get a family photo during the home visit so this can be on display when the children start nursery. This again helps them feel welcome.

Home visit checklist

- Contact form (includes medical information) _____
- Form detailing who can collect the child _____
- Ethnicity form (ensure completed) _____
- Local trip permission letter _____
- Booklet explained & copy left with family _____
- Start date and sessions explained _____
- Photo of child _____
- Photo of family _____

Figure 1.2 Home visit checklist

For the benefit of the child, we take along toys, books, paper, pencils and scissors as well as photos of the school and nursery. If the child is relaxed and confident, this can become a perfect opportunity to assess the child's personality, interests and abilities. This information can be vital to ensure that the nursery will meet their needs. For example, this year Arda was fascinated by the scissors and spent the whole visit cutting up any piece of paper he was given. He had never used scissors before but clearly loved the experience. Once he started nursery he did not settle easily, but the scissors were the one thing that enticed him to engage and stay willingly at the nursery. Other children often joined him in this activity and therefore several children developed their scissor skills!

One important aspect of the home visit is to inform the family about a start date and how the induction process works. Once we have met the children we are able to put them into groups for various start dates. We usually opt to start the shy or young children first so that they experience the nursery when it is quiet and not too crowded. After the visits we are in a position to decide if we feel any child will need individual support and in extreme cases we can delay the start date until this is in place. Last year, for example, when we arrived for one visit, it was clear that the child would need specialist provision. During the visit it also became clear that the parents thought we were from a special school. Once the situation was clarified, we were able to advise the parents and avoid unnecessary confusion for the child.

We give the children in nursery the option of wearing a 'uniform' and take sweatshirts and book bags along with us for the parents to purchase if they wish. This year many families have opted to dress their child in the uniform – it certainly means fewer arguments over clothing in the mornings!

Setting up the environment

An enabling environment

In the remaining chapters of the book, various areas of the class and garden are described in detail. However, here I will outline the general principals that have been applied in the planning and organisation of the environment. Although various aspects of the environment are described in each chapter, the whole environment is set up and stocked before the children start nursery. This is essential so that the children can be trained in how to use the various areas from day one. As stated in the Introduction, the environment is one piece of the jigsaw – a perfect environment without all the other components will not create an outstanding nursery. However a nursery without an outstanding environment will not be an outstanding nursery either. It is a very important piece of the picture and that is why it is given such prominence in this book. If the environment is perfect, all children can be fully engaged in purposeful play of their own choice and interest.

We have a **workshop** setup both indoors and outside. This means that in all areas, the resources are available and accessible to the children at all times, but nothing is set out. So, therefore, **the tables are clear at the start of the day**, the sand and water are free of equipment (but the resources are available next to these areas), the playdough is in its container on the shelf, the PE equipment is in its usual position at the edge of the area, etc.

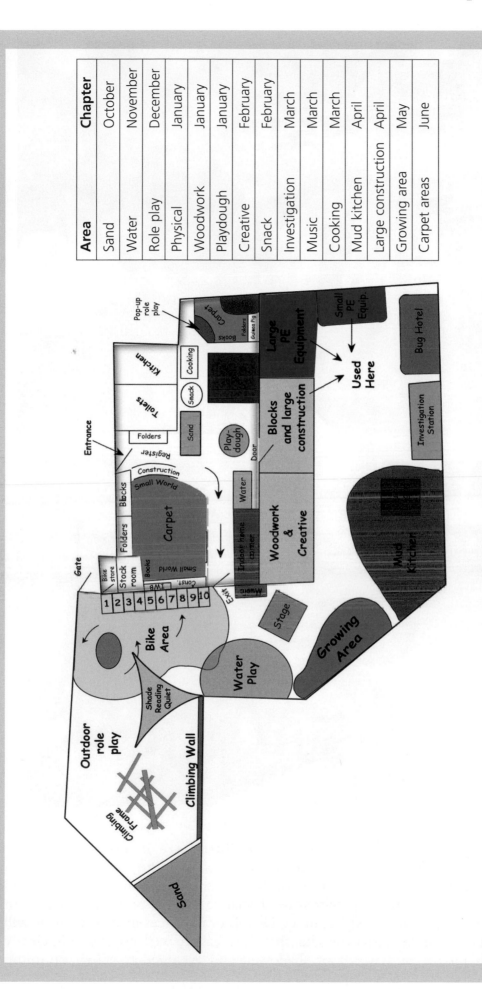

Area	Chapter
Sand	October
Water	November
Role play	December
Physical	January
Woodwork	January
Playdough	January
Creative	February
Snack	February
Investigation	March
Music	March
Cooking	March
Mud kitchen	April
Large construction	April
Growing area	May
Carpet areas	June

Figure 1.3 Plan of class and garden

When a class is organised in this way, **the children are in control of their learning**. They are able to select the area in which to play, the resources to use in that area and what to do with them. Obviously their choices are limited by the areas and resources available and it is therefore crucial to have appropriate areas with varied, high-quality, open-ended resources. Details of resources in various areas will be covered in each chapter. It is also vital that the areas are well stocked, tidy, clearly labelled (with picture and word) or shadowed and arranged to allow optimum access. Each cohort of children will be different and their interests and curiosities will change over the period of the year. We constantly review and reflect on the environment to see which areas are proving productive and which need altering. For example, early in the term we realised that the children were often using the water toys in the dry sand because the positioning was confusing. We rearranged the class so that the two areas were further apart. This removed the confusion and the resources were then used correctly.

Another example was the outdoor construction equipment that was in a different area to the building site resources. The staff realised that the children wanted to combine the resources and they therefore moved the building site resources. The play immediately became more productive and the resources were used more often.

Similarly the resources are assessed and reviewed constantly with changes made as necessary. For example, we noticed how several children liked to talk on the toy telephones indoors and so we bought some telephones for outdoors so that the children who played predominantly outdoors also had access to this resource.

The second telephone is at the other end of this bush – the children can't see each other when talking on the phones – making the experience more exciting.

Because the children select and access resources themselves, they know where they are from and they know where to put them back when they have finished using them or at the end of the session. Shadowing resources is used to aid this process – for example as seen below with the indoor blocks. The shadows are cut from coloured card or paper and glued to the shelf. Once covered in sticky-back plastic, the shadowing will remain in place for several years – a task worth doing! This is a very time-consuming task but once complete, the unit will stay tidy and the resources are valued and cared for.

Outdoors, it takes only five minutes to set up the garden. This is because as many resources as possible are left in position, though if they are likely to be damaged by rain, then they are covered with tarpaulins, secured at night with elasticated rope. A video of the nursery garden being set up is viewable at www.freedomtolearn.co.uk/links.

Indoors, it takes a short time to set up as well – the water tray has to be filled up and the snacks prepared. Staff spend the period before nursery restocking and checking resources. As you can see in the picture on page 14, the tables are clear at the start of the session. Staff do not spend time setting resources out on the tables.

If you look back to the timetable for September, you will see '2 days preparing class and garden'. During these two days, the whole nursery team is available to carry out tasks in the class and garden – for example shadowing, labelling resources, preparing coat pegs, organising folders, painting outdoor units if necessary etc. The work done on these days means that when the children arrive, the environment is ready and as good as it can possibly be. I have an on-going wish list and it is on these days that some things on that list can be crossed off. If you plan to approach your senior managers to ask for this valuable time, then you need to be sure to have an action plan prepared. Be clear about how the time will be used and how the work will benefit the children. Make sure you are aware of cost implications as well. Many tasks just require time, such as digging over some soil to create a mini-beast area or reorganising the layout of the class. Other tasks require minimal expense: covering units with tarpaulins or sorting plastic resources into shopping baskets. More expensive items will probably require a written bid to have been presented the summer before. Start your wish list and add to it as you read through this book, then prioritise and calculate some costs. The more organised and thoughtful you appear, the more likely you are to get agreement from your managers.

As the home visits are completed, staff have confirmed spellings of names and what children want to be called. They also have photos of each child and can then prepare labels for pegs, folders, register and the mark-making area. There are many ways to do self-registration. This year Jacqui opted to have circular labels. The children collect their name from the entrance to nursery (where it is attached with Velcro), carry it into nursery and stick it onto a board inside the room.

It is vital that the register and peg labels are prepared before the first children arrive. Staff and parents can then train the children how to self-register and how to find their own peg from day one.

Induction

Once all the home visits are complete, the children come into nursery in groups. Each child attends for two sessions in their first week and then the number of sessions is increased each week, if appropriate. We have devised a list of criteria (see Figure 1.4) for the children to meet before their number of sessions will be increased to five.

The child should be able to:

1. Separate from carer easily.
2. Move independently around the garden and class.
3. Stay awake and energetic throughout the session.
4. Behave appropriately (and non-aggressively) for the majority of the time.
5. Attempt to manage their own personal hygiene.

Figure 1.4 Criteria to stay for a full week in nursery

The first few days

Some children will settle very quickly into nursery and are willing to be left within a few minutes of arriving. Others will take much, much longer to feel confident. Some children will want a parent around, even if they are settled. The main message is that every child is unique and they will settle in their own time and their own way. The staff are constantly assessing the children and discussing with the parents if they think it is appropriate for the child to be left. The most important aspect of this process is that the children are aware of what is happening. They need to know that if their parent is leaving, then they will be back soon. A visual timetable can help to reassure the children and can be used when the parent has left, even if the child has no English.

In the afternoon the clock photos are changed to 12.30 and 3.30. Children arrive between 12.30 pm and 1 pm in the afternoon.

The session routine can be seen from this timetable and it is very simple. The three hours in the afternoon are organised in exactly the same way. The children can arrive at any time between 8.30 and 9.00 am. They self-register and then they have a long period (well over two and a half hours) in which to explore, play and learn. The doors to the garden are open from 8.30 am as well and many children don't even bother to take their coat off – they just go straight out to the garden. Tidying up takes about 5 minutes, the circle time is about 10 minutes (and will be increased to 20 minutes over the course of the year), and then the children are collected.

Some children will settle almost immediately and their parents will be able to leave them for complete sessions within a few days. For children who are unsure, the settling pattern is usually as follows. Their parent will stay with them and play with them for a few sessions. This will ensure that they know their way around the nursery and its routines and they know what they enjoy doing. Then there will be a few sessions when we encourage the parent to stay in the room, but to just sit in clear view of the child

For some children, it is a good idea to ask parents to sit in the classroom reading and in view of their child, but not interacting with them. In this way the child gains confidence to go off and play, secure in the knowledge that their parent is staying put!

without giving them too much attention. Then the parent will start leaving the room for short periods and return before the session end. Finally they will be able to leave for the whole session. If a child is unsure and this routine is followed, then they will usually settle and be completely relaxed within a few weeks. A few weeks can seem like a long time, but it is well worth the investment.

Unfortunately there are always a few parents who think that because their child is playing happily, then it is fine to slip out of the nursery without saying anything to the child (or to the staff!). However, once the child realises they have been left, the distress and fear are immense. In these cases, we have to ring a parent to return and the settling process will inevitably take much longer once the child has lost trust in the adults.

Other children may be used to controlling their parents, and will be keen for them to stay. In some cases the staff will decide that the child is fine and will explain that their parent is leaving and will be back soon. Sometimes the child will get very angry, but this is not the same as being distressed or scared and it is a tricky judgement call. Staff and parents must be in agreement before the decision is made for any parent to leave.

Many children accept the boundaries and expectations in the nursery immediately. For others, the main focus of the teaching in the first few weeks is the establishment of these boundaries and expectations. Occasional tantrums will occur and *Mercury's Child* (Dyer, 2007) comes to mind. Some children are able to get exactly what they want at home by using various strategies. In nursery, we have to be careful to show that some things are non-negotiable, regardless of how angry it makes the child. For example a boy who wanted to leave his coat in the middle of the nursery floor found it very difficult to accept that this was not going to happen. In such cases, we need to be calm and clear in our response – it is not a time for negotiation: 'You need to hang your coat up on your peg'. In this instance it took quite a while before the boy complied. The parent also had to be stopped from picking the coat up for the child and they needed reassurance that it was ok for the child to be a bit angry. Once the coat was on the peg we were able to distract the child and move on to one of the many wonderful things that the nursery has to offer. In this case, the watering cans were the perfect distraction and the coat was forgotten. This is also the time to ensure that the few expectations are adhered to at all times. So we insist that the children will not hurt each other, that indoors they will walk and use quiet voices and that everywhere they will tidy away resources once they have finished with them. Parents can be a great help during the first few sessions, to make sure that their children understand these rules and adhere to them. Much of the learning and development in the first weeks centres around these personal and social skills. Once established, the nursery will be a much calmer, safer and happier place for all the children. They can then get on with the serious business of playing and exploring to learn and develop. Once all children are clear about the expectations, then a 'zero tolerance' approach is established – ensuring clear, consistent messages are given. Having been a foster carer for ten years, I have learnt just how often some children will test the boundaries. Each time that the boundaries are re-established, the child will feel more and more secure (and the staff feel more and more exasperated!). A 'time-out' spot is used quickly and consistently, giving the child as little attention as possible. The message they are getting is that 'in nursery, this is the rule and it will always be the rule'. Although this may appear harsh, it is the quickest and kindest way to help the children understand that nursery is a predictable, safe place in which they can relax and play and that the chaos or inconsistency that some of them may experience at home will not happen at nursery.

During the induction period, parents can be a valuable help – explaining rules and expectations to the children and supporting them to adhere to these. In this photo we see a mum supporting her child as they have their first attempt at hammering nails.

Conflict resolution

As stated, the main teaching at this time of year centres around PSE skills to create a nursery in which the children are safe, happy and confident. The rules and boundaries are a large part of this but we also need the children to be as independent as possible. This includes all the self-care routines of coats, boots, toileting, accessing and using resources appropriately, eating and drinking. However, one main area of focus is teaching the children to be independent in their dealings with each other. For example, if Mira snatches a toy from Ali, an adult will join the pair, give the toy back to Ali and then speak to Mira saying 'if you want that toy, you need to ask Ali – so speak to her and say "Can I have that toy please?"'. The adult will also then speak to Ali and say 'You don't have to give her the toy – you can say "No, I am using it". Or you might say "You can have it in a minute"'. The adult will then encourage the pair to talk like this and resolve the dispute. If a child is upset because another child has shouted at them, the adult will again model a response and encourage the child to use it saying, for example: 'Don't shout at me. I don't like it'. It is not very helpful to say to children 'you need to share' or 'play nicely' as they don't know what that means. They need specific language such as 'You have it for 3 minutes and then I will have it for 3 minutes' (using a timer perhaps) or 'You have all 4 trains and I am sad because I have none. Can you give me some?'. If the children can come up with solutions for themselves, they will be more likely to find a solution the next time without calling on an adult. This level of independence is so valuable and allows the adults to move on to teaching in other areas of development.

Once the children have learnt how to negotiate about turn-taking, then they don't need to call on adults in situations like this. They talk to each other and come to an agreement.

Makaton

Many of our children have little English, a few have language delay and some are very shy. For all the children, the use of Makaton signing is a fantastic way to help their communication skills to develop. It is also a great way to get simple messages across to everyone. We introduce simple signs from day one and encourage the parents to help the children learn the signs at home – toilet, walking, stop, sit down, look, hello, help, please, thank you – if everyone can 'say' and understand these words, the settling process is made that little bit easier.

Diary extracts: Examples of development and learning

WHAT TO LOOK OUT FOR

- The children are familiar with the staff and the nursery setting.
- Resources in the nursery reflect the interests of the children.
- Support is in place for any children with additional needs.
- Most children are happy and confident in the nursery.
- Most parents are confident to leave their children in the nursery.
- Resources are accessed easily and independently.
- Children explore all areas and begin to take risks and try new experiences.
- Children make new friends.
- Children learn the class routines and expectations.
- Children begin to manage conflicts and negotiations independently.
- Some children demonstrate high levels of involvement for sustained periods.

With up to 46 children in the nursery at any one time, I could fill a book with the learning that happens every day. I will try to select the most typical events each month and explain the learning that was occurring.

Water play

The warm weather means that most children are opting to be outside and they can enjoy the various activities involving water, without getting too cold. A few children suggested washing the bikes and Jacqui pointed out where the sponges and buckets were located and reminded the children about wearing aprons. The children chose their sponges and buckets, filled the buckets with water from the butt and then washed several bikes. Soon the windows were being cleaned too. Three children, who were reluctant to join in, stood and watched for a long time and with encouragement, they eventually helped to clean the windows.

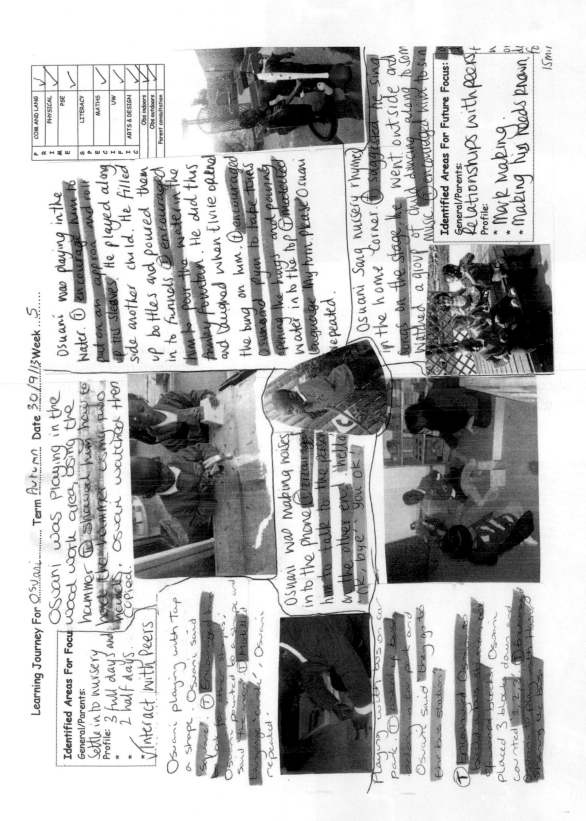

Figure 1.5 Sample learning journey for September

Note: See Chapter 2: October for explanation.

The children learnt that they will be supported to pursue new ideas, shown where some resources were kept, that they need to wear aprons, how to use a window scraper, properties of sponges and water, how to negotiate turn-taking, what the size and shapes of the windows felt like and that a new experience might be fun!

Several children were enjoying filling watering cans and watering the vegetable plot. Rachel explained how the different plants had different shaped leaves. She encouraged Eren to pull up a carrot and then the group discussed what they should do with the carrot. Eventually they agreed to feed it to the guinea pigs. The adults explained that the children should only give food to the guinea pigs if an adult has said that it is ok. Eren was thrilled when the guinea pig tugged the carrot out of his hand.

The children learnt that carrots grow in the ground, that different vegetable plants have different leaves, that guinea pigs like to eat carrots and that we have to be careful about what we feed the guinea pigs.

Moving 1 tonne of soil

A cubic metre of soil was delivered into the car park for the extension to the vegetable patch. The children watched the lorry unload the bag and then the group discussed how to get the soil into the nursery garden. Several children suggested using the wheelbarrows and over the course of the day, the whole bag of soil was transported into the new area.

The children learnt how a wheelbarrow is used and how it feels when it is empty and full, how to negotiate sharing resources, how to keep safe when a large lorry is manoeuvring, how soil feels, looks and smells. They also learnt that they can move 1 tonne of soil!

Work or Play?
Children do not distinguish between the two.
Play is a serious business.

Introduction to woodwork and cakes

Several children were making cakes in the sand. Jacqui encouraged them to decorate their cakes with buttons that they found in the sand. The group discussed how to make real cakes and Jacqui suggested they could do that in nursery. Once the children realised that there were no ingredients in the class, then a trip to the shop was essential. The cake was made on their return and shared among the class at the end of the session.

The children learnt so much from this sequence of events. Possibly the most important thing was that the nursery is an exciting, supportive and safe place to be, with endless possibilities. Each child will have gained something different because for each child different parts of the day were important to them. We can never be 100 per cent sure about what they have learnt. That is why teaching in the early years is so fascinating – and for many, quite daunting.

The woodwork bench is proving popular and it is still necessary to have an adult nearby at all times. Gradually all the children are showing an interest and as they do so, the adults are on hand to make sure that they know the rules and expectations. Several children are already skilled at hammering in nails without injuring their fingers.

Woodwork is discussed at length in the Chapter 5: January.

The activities that have occurred during September are recorded by the staff on 'planning' sheets. This process is described in more detail in the next chapter.

As September comes to an end, it is clear that the children are already beginning to trust in their nursery. This is evident in their willingness to explore, their relaxed behaviour and their obvious enjoyment. This does not happen by accident – the environment is meeting their needs and catering to their interests and the staff are interacting skilfully to ensure that every possible learning opportunity is captured and developed. The year is off to a wonderful start.

2 October

Over the course of the month of October, the majority of children will begin to attend their full sessions without a parent. They will be mixing with a large group of children and several adults each day. For their experience to be safe and happy, every aspect of the nursery needs to be well organised and every member of staff must know exactly what they should be doing. The month is very hard work for the staff (both physically and emotionally) as the children are still so young and so new to the setting. The half-term break is always very welcome. In this chapter, I explain the weekly routines, including the system of 'focus children', 'in the moment planning' and record keeping (including initial assessments). In the environment section, I describe the sand areas indoors and outside. The diary is full of wonderful examples of links with parents, surprising achievements and trips into the local area.

OCTOBER: TO DO LIST

- Ensure staff are clear about their roles.
- Continue to establish expectations and ground rules.
- Complete initial assessments.
- Continue recording the learning and development of groups.
- Start the first cycle of focus children.
- Start the first cycle of parent meetings.
- Reflect on and amend the nursery environment.
- Update individual folders.

The weekly routine: Focus children and parental involvement

On Friday each week we select the 'focus children' for the following week. This is 10 per cent of the class – so in our nursery that is six children – three in the morning and three in the afternoon. Each child must be a focus child once per term. At the beginning of the year we tend to choose children who have settled quickly, show good levels of involvement and appear quite confident. There are many reasons for this: they will be able to cope with some close attention; they are confident enough for staff to give them some appropriate challenges; also their learning journey sheet (see Appendix B and Figure 2.7 on page 44) will be completed quite quickly and this is important at this early stage of the year

Planning for your child's learning journey

Next week we will be focusing on _____ We will be observing them while they play to find out more about their interests and how they are progressing. Please take some pictures (**no more than 15**) of your child/family enjoying activities out of school.

We value the knowledge and understanding you have of your child and would really appreciate it if you would share this with us so that together we can plan activities to meet your child's needs. This will help us plan for their future learning and development.

Is there anything significant happening in your child's life at the moment e.g. visits, holidays, new pets, family celebrations? Is there anything you would like to tell us about your child?

Do you have anything you would like to ask us about your child's progress and development?

Please return this sheet with the school camera by _____ so that we can add your thoughts and ideas to the planning process. Please ensure that the camera is used with adult supervision, kept away from water and no objects are places on the cameras LED screen. **If your child would like to bring something to show to the class, please send that to school one day next week.** Thank you,

Carterhatch

Infant School • Children's Centres

Figure 2.1 Parent consultation sheet

because the staff still have to work hard with the settling of many of the other children. Once the children have been selected, they are given a parent consultation sheet to take home (see Figure 2.1) and also a digital camera. We speak to the parents and explain that we would like them to fill in the sheet in as much detail as possible and also to take some photos over the weekend. There are two examples of completed parent sheets in Figures 2.2 and 2.3.

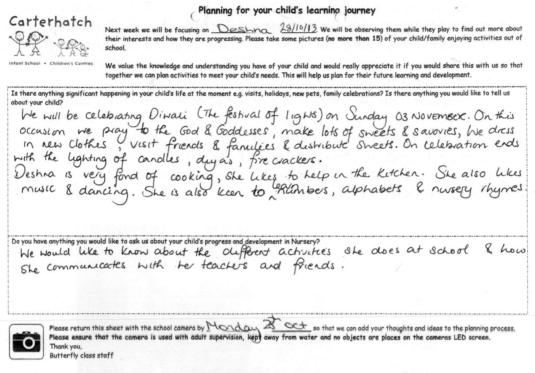

Figure 2.2 Completed parent consultation sheet 1

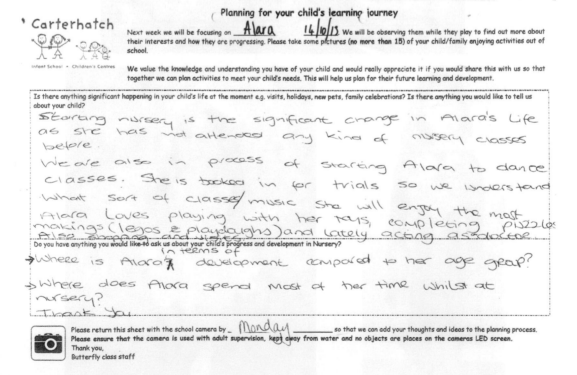

Figure 2.3 Completed parent consultation sheet 2

The consultation sheets and the cameras are returned after the weekend. The information provided by the parents is fascinating and we often find out about events that the child might never have revealed – visiting relatives, family events, new pets etc. The completed sheets are stored in the child's folder – a lovely example of the parents' voice. The photos will often link to this information and can prompt the child to talk about these things. A colleague who introduced the cameras in her nursery was delighted when a girl brought the camera back with photos of two pigs that were living in her garden! This child had never spoken in nursery, but the genuine fascination of the staff, and the child's expert knowledge of pigs, meant that she felt able to talk about them. Once her confidence was boosted by this event, she carried on speaking regularly in nursery. This year the most noticeable things in the first few lots of photos are that many children get involved with cooking at home, several have musical instruments and several go to places of worship on a regular basis. We print some of the photos from each child to put in their folder (see Chapter 3: November) and note down anything that the child says about the pictures. As the year progresses and the group settles, we also show some of the photos on the interactive whiteboard, allowing other children in the group to see the pictures. If they are able, we encourage the child to talk about the photos as they are shown and an adult writes down exactly what they say.

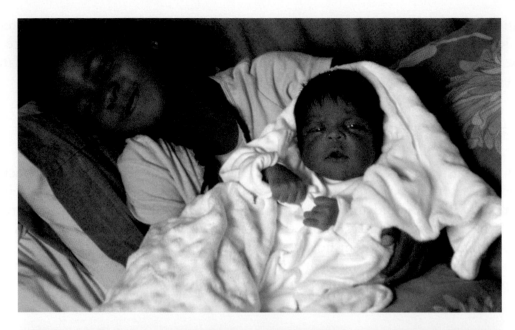

Learning journey sheets for the focus children

On Monday one learning journey sheet is put up on the planning board for each of the focus children (see Appendix B). These sheets are blank at the start of the week, except for the name, date and a couple of notes to remind staff about any particular areas that we wish to focus on with the child and anything that the parents have asked us about. You can find an example of a completed learning journey in this and each following chapter of the book.

In the Introduction, I explained the theory behind this approach. In brief, we have set up an enabling environment that is the best we can possibly have and we encourage the children to explore and learn by pursuing their own interests. The staff observe and inter-act with the children in their pursuits – looking out for 'teachable moments' in which they can make a difference. Such interactions with the focus children are then recorded on the learning journeys. All adults who interact with a focus child contribute to the learning journeys. This process contains a moment in which the adult has to 'plan' what to do as a result of what they have observed.

Planning in the moment

In many settings, observations are made, the plans are written down and the activity is delivered at a later date. We do not do any such forward planning – rather we remain 'in the moment' with the child and respond immediately. If a child is concentrating on using a hammer at 2 pm on Monday, that is the moment in which a skilful adult can interact with that child and 'teach' them how to use the hammer effectively. The child is motivated and interested in that moment and therefore keen to learn. Such an interaction might appear on a learning journey as follows ('T' indicates 'adult'):

> Alara was trying to hammer in a nail but it kept falling over. T modelled how to hold the nail between thumb and finger and tap gently. Alara watched carefully and then copied the technique correctly. The nail stayed upright and Alara was then able to hammer it firmly.

We highlight the 'teaching' in yellow and **it is vital that the entries on the learning journeys do contain an element of teaching**. Observations, without any 'plan' or 'teaching' are recorded but not included on the learning journeys – rather they are stored separately in the child's individual folder.

Another example might read:

> Nadir was struggling to cut a piece of tape. T modelled how to use the dispenser and pointed out the blade. Nadir persevered to try and cut the tape. T praised his efforts and encouraged him to keep trying. Eventually Nadir was delighted to cut a piece of tape himself.

I visit many settings and often see plans for focused activities related to the teaching of sharing and turn-taking. However, it is far more powerful to do this teaching at a moment when it is relevant to the children in a real situation. For example an entry on Kai's learning journey reads:

> Kai wanted a go on the bike. 'I' modelled the phrase and Kai repeated 'Can I have a turn please?'. 'I' encouraged Kai to say this to the boy on the bike. Kai did so and the boy gave the bike to Kai. The two boys then took turns independently.

In all these examples, the children made progress in a very short space of time. Whenever anyone is observing in the early years, I try to be with them in order to point out the progress being made and the 'teaching' that enabled the progress to happen. I am often asked about 'next steps' and how these are noted/remembered. I point out that when working 'in the moment', the next steps are carried out immediately and therefore we do not need to record them anywhere else. I have visited many settings where they have written down literally hundreds of 'next steps' and the staff are stressed trying to remember them all and trying to find time to teach them!

Figure 2.4 shows the traditional teaching cycle that is recognised as best practice. The timescale for the duration of the cycle is where our 'in the moment' practice differs from the majority of settings. We complete the whole cycle hundreds of times each day (some of which are recorded), whereas in other settings the cycle is spread over a day or a week, with observations happening one day and the resulting activity happening the next day or the next week.

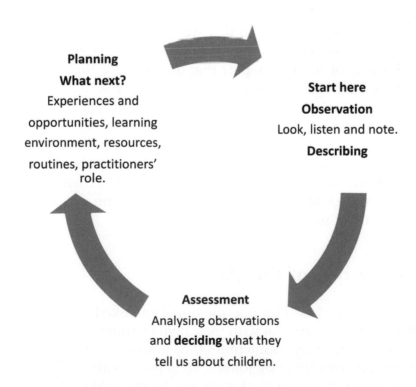

Planning
What next?
Experiences and opportunities, learning environment, resources, routines, practitioners' role.

Start here
Observation
Look, listen and note.
Describing

Assessment
Analysing observations and **deciding** what they tell us about children.

Figure 2.4 The traditional teaching cycle

However it is recognised that to respond immediately is the most powerful way to teach our youngest children. The National Strategies document, *Learning, Playing and Interacting*, states:

> Babies and young children … are experiencing and learning in the here and now, not storing up their questions until tomorrow or next week. It is in that moment of curiosity, puzzlement, effort or interest – the 'teachable moment' – that the skilful adult makes a difference. By using this cycle on a moment-by-moment basis, the adult will be always alert to individual children (observation), always thinking about what it tells us about the child's thinking (assessment), and always ready to respond by using appropriate strategies at the right moment to support children's well-being and learning (planning for the next moment).
>
> (Department for Children, Schools and Families, 2009: 22–23)

This is exactly what we do throughout every session in nursery and reception. The *Evaluation Schedule for Inspections* has a useful quote too:

> Teaching should not be taken to imply a 'top down' or formal way of working. It is a broad term which covers the many different ways in which adults help young children learn. It includes their interactions with children during planned and child-initiated play and activities: communicating and modelling language, showing, explaining, demonstrating, exploring ideas, encouraging, questioning, recalling, providing a narrative for what they are doing, facilitating and setting challenges.
>
> (OFSTED, 2014: 7)

These are exactly the sorts of things that we record on our learning journeys.

We often take a photo of the events and these are added to the learning journey as well. By the end of the week, the sheet is full of notes and photos – a unique record of that child's learning and development in that week. An example of a completed sheet is shown in Figure 2.7 and further examples appear in each chapter of the book. Teachers who have tried this way of working report that not only are they re-inspired and happy in their role, they have also got to know the children very well and as unique individuals. The teacher keeps a colour copy of each learning journey in her planning file and the original copy goes in the child's folder.

In the week following their focus week, we invite the parents of the child into nursery for a discussion about the week and all that we have learnt about the child. We discuss any points that the parents have written on the consultation form and encourage them to add comments to the child's folder. Together we agree on possible areas for focus in future and how we can all support the child with these.

Planning for the rest of the class

What about the rest of the class? This is a question I am asked over and over. The answer is simple. The other children carry on with their own learning journeys (even though they are not recorded in the same way). Sometimes they journey on their own, sometimes with a friend or a group and sometimes by joining an activity with one of the focus children. Also the adults are not totally absorbed with the focus children – this would be overwhelming for those children. The adults are often free to support other individuals or groups. We use a separate A3 sheet to record activities involving a group (see Appendix

C). Again, this is started on a Monday and completed during the week. We may end up with three or four of these sheets by the end of the week. The sheet is designed to record the whole teaching cycle: observation; assessment and plan; teaching; and observation/outcome. An example of a completed sheet is shown in Figure 2.8. Further examples appear in the book. We continually review this sheet and amend it according to staff ideas. One such amendment is evident in the sheets that appear later in the book, with a new heading appearing in the final column. Children's names do not appear on these sheets – they are a record of a group activity when an adult has been involved and had an impact.

We call these sheets 'Planning in the moment'. As with the individual children, staff will look out for activities or events that have captured the interest of a group. They will join the group to see if they can support, enhance or develop the activity in any way. Thus they are observing and assessing. Sometimes the group is operating independently and with deep-level involvement (see Introduction) and any attempt to join the activity might actually disrupt it. In this situation the adult may observe for a while, possibly taking particular note of some children and then move away. However, on many occasions a skilful adult will spot a 'teachable moment'. They then decide what to do – this is **planning**. They might provide an extra resource, an idea, some vocabulary, some information or they might model a skill or demonstrate how to use a piece of equipment – this is **teaching**.

Figure 2.5 shows how an entry might read:

Observation (and assessment)	(Plan and) teaching	Outcome (observation)
Children attempting to build a tent by placing fabric on tepee frame. (Children are unaware of how to use pegs.)	'T' showed the children the box of pegs and modelled how to use them to secure the fabric in place.	The tent was then built by the group.

Figure 2.5 Entry in a 'Planning in the moment' sheet

This den frame was made simply by screwing lengths of wood together and then attaching Ikea rails so that it is easy to attach the fabric with pegs. The salt bin at the back of the den is ideal for storing the fabric, carpet pieces, pegs, string, etc. that are needed for successful building.

With all this wonderful teaching, the children soon start to do things independently and when such moments are observed we refer to them as 'Wow!' moments – see Chapter 3: November for details.

Initial assessments

For each child we need to make some initial assessments. This a requirement of OFSTED, although it does **not** specify the format or method that is to be used. The requirement is that practitioners are aware of whether their children are operating well below, below, at, above or well above the expected level. The 'expected level' is whatever is appropriate for their age – i.e. if they are 36 months old, they should be at a developmental level appropriate for a child aged 36 months. The difficulty arises when you try to define what that level is. The vast majority of settings use Early Education's *Development Matters* (2012) (or the extracted part of that which is called 'Early Years Outcomes') but there is **no statutory requirement** to use this document or any other. You do, however, need to be able to explain how you have assessed the children on entry. OFSTED guidance to inspectors states that they should find out the proportions in each group (well below, below, etc.) on entry. At the time of writing this, I have been through four inspections in the last six years and I have not been required to break down the assessments into any great detail – they accept an 'average' for each child. I would, however, recommend keeping detailed raw data that can be referred to if necessary.

With this in mind, we assess PSE, communication and language and physical development on entry to nursery (at present these are referred to as the 'Prime Areas of Development'). The staff make their assessments based on their interactions and observations of the children during their first few weeks in nursery. We try to get to know the children as well as possible in this time so that the assessments are as accurate as possible. The school uses a commercial package for data tracking and the data are entered into the computer and analysed. The programme is able to analyse according to gender, term of birth, English as an additional language (EAL) etc. This information can be useful but I am very wary about grouping children at such a young age. Two Turkish summer-born boys are two unique individuals and should be treated as individuals, with a unique life story and unique interests and needs. We do the best for each and every child, regardless of which group they happen to fit into. The entry data summary for this year is shown in Figure 2.6.

Nursery	% well below expected level	% below expected level	% at expected level	% above expected level
Entry (September 2013)	37	43	15	5

Figure 2.6 Entry data summarised for OFSTED

Setting up the environment

Sand area outdoors

Top tip: Laminating
The labels above these baskets have been up for over a year. The secret to long-lasting labels is to ensure that the laminating sheet is much bigger than the picture – about 3 cms all round is good. Then when you staple the picture up, make sure that the staples go through the clear laminating sheet and not through the paper. If you staple through the paper, the rain will get in the first day that it rains. Staple through the clear sheet and your labels will last all year and beyond.

This area is one of the most popular outdoors. Our sandpit is built from treated sleepers and I have made similar structures in numerous settings. The sleepers are relatively cheap to buy and can be placed directly onto a hard surface. Fixings are not essential as the sleepers are so heavy that small children cannot usually move them. Washed silver sand is ideal to fill the area and then resources need to be stored nearby. We have attached metal shopping baskets to the fence – just hooked onto cup hooks – with a photo and word above each basket to help with tidying up. These baskets are fantastic as they can be left out all the time – the resources are plastic and the rain goes through the baskets. The baskets contain buckets, spades, vehicles, moulds, sieves and natural resources (shells, conkers, twigs, stones, bark etc.). Close by is another unit with plates, cutlery, saucepans etc. for the inevitable cooking that takes place, along with a small table and chairs to promote role play. We have attached pulleys to the fence and a large hanging balance as well as an 'easy easel' rail for mark-making. The sand pit is covered with a tarpaulin at night – held in place with tyres placed on top. The sand outdoors is usually wet – either from the rain or from water transported to the area by the children. This allows for sand castles, volcanoes, tunnels, rivers and mountains etc. to be built. We observe high levels of involvement in this area – children are fascinated by sand, its properties and its potential. When I visit other settings, I often advise practitioners to spend a day in the sand pit – observe the children carefully in their play and find out why they are so fascinated.

Setting up the environment

Sand indoors

The sand indoors is equally popular but is contained in a much smaller unit. We keep this sand dry and have fewer resources available. The storage unit can be seen here with shadowing on the higher shelves and baskets on the bottom shelf. The staff constantly review the nursery environment and the resources in the baskets can be changed if the levels of involvement drop or if a particular interest emerges. Usually the baskets contain natural resources (shells, stones, twigs etc.) and cups, plates and cutlery. The shadowed resources are various sizes and shapes and there is also a balance and a sand wheel. 'Less is more' in this case – a varied selection of items ensures the sand is used purposefully.

Diary extracts: Examples of development and learning

WHAT TO LOOK OUT FOR

- The majority of children are staying for their full five sessions.
- Ground rules and expectations are established.
- The children are exploring the whole environment and using all the resources.
- The learning journeys show that the children are making progress in many areas.
- Initial assessments are complete.

It is always difficult to select events to include in the diary section. What has been particularly noticeable this month has been the enthusiasm shown for the activities that might not be available at home, for example keeping a pet, woodwork and large-scale building. There are also some lovely examples of child-initiated activities being extended and developed when adults observe carefully and make sensitive suggestions. When I am asked how we ensure a balance between child-initiated and adult-directed activities, I point out events such as these. All our activities are child-initiated, but adults always get involved if they see learning potential that the children might not access independently.

Guinea pigs

We have two guinea pigs in the nursery and while some children are keen to hold them, others are happy just to sit nearby and maybe stroke them. Empathy is developing and the children regularly check that the water bottle is full and that there is food in the bowl.

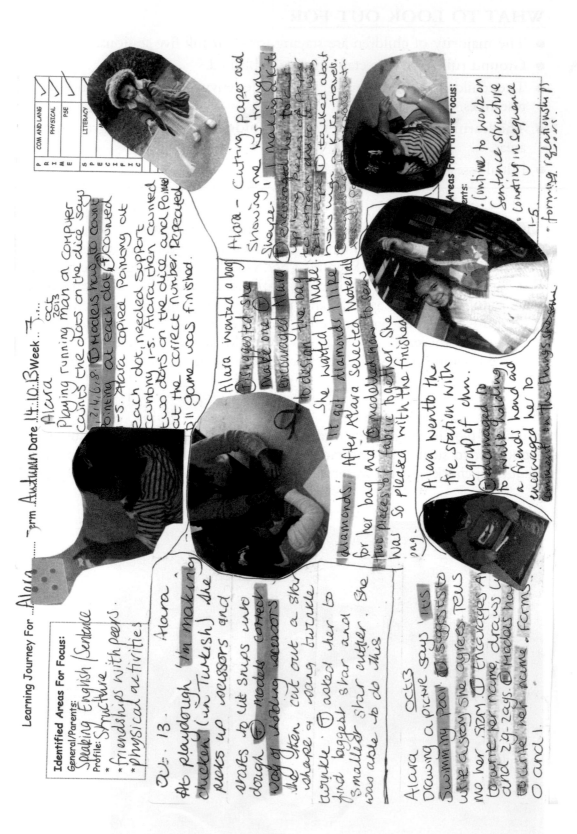

Figure 2.7 Sample learning journey for October

Note: See above for explanation.

Carterhatch
Infant School • Children's Centre

In the moment Planning - Nursery

Week commencing: 23rd Sept 2013

Day	Observation	Action Taken	Next Steps (if appropriate)
① 23.9.13 SA	Children using wooden snail as a car. Children say "we've broke down. we need a mechanic."	⊤ Supported children + encouraged use of tools + tyres – pretended to be mechanics.	
② 24/9/13	Children wanted to react the three little pigs in the garden	⊤ supported them in to getting into the wigwam to use as the house and I was the wolf	Read story at carpet session.
③ 24/9/13 SA	Children junk modelling – tell me – "I'm making a house." "I need windows and a door."	⊤ Encouraged use of all resources – Spoke about what their houses look like – how many windows, door number etc. (photos)	
④ Tue JG	Chn playing with cars ⊤ spoke to chn about her new car.	⊤ Showed them around the car talking about Petrol, wheels etc. ⊤ then encouraged chn to make cars at the woodwork bench.	Show completed models to class at carpet time.
⑤ Tue PP	Chn finding hard to settle	⊤ Encouraged chn to look at the pictures and talk about their families with their peers.	
⑥ Tue B.	Chn playing fishing game some ch wanted all fish. ⊤ encouraged them to take turns fishing for fish	⊤ modelled how to take turns getting a fish each.	Observe this area to see if share independently tomorrow.

Photos

Figure 2.8 Sample 'Planning in the moment' sheet

Note: See above for explanation.

Woodwork

More children have now accessed the woodwork area. We still have an adult nearby but the children are already clear about the rules and expectations – 'only two children at a time and protective goggles must be worn'. (Detailed discussion about woodwork is in Chapter 5: January). Many children have made considerable progress in their hand–eye coordination and in their ability to hit the nails with force.

Large-scale construction

The large-scale construction area (see details in Chapter 8: April) has been in constant use lately. On several occasions the children have built bridges and staff have encouraged them to use the bridges as part of the 'Billy Goat Gruff' story.

Child initiated/adult guided

A group of children were smelling the leaves in the growing area and an adult said that they could pick some. The children then discussed what they could do with the leaves and Jacqui suggested they could make scented necklaces. She modelled how to use a needle and thread to create a necklace. The group were excited and engaged in this activity and indeed the next day, some of them made another necklace independently.

Several children were role playing fire fighters in the garden. Discussion revealed that some of the group had never seen a real fire engine. Since the fire station is only about a quarter of a mile from school, a group walked down to see the real thing. Luckily, the fire fighters were not busy and could not resist the curious faces of the children peering through their windows. They let them into the station, showed them around, demonstrated how they slide down the pole and let the children sit in the fire engine!

Once back at school some of the children were keen to make a fire engine at the wood-work bench.

Some children have a keen interest in cars and Daniel is among this group. In the week when he was a focus child he was involved in making cars in the large construction area, leading to a discussion about engines and repairs, leading to a visit to see some real cars in the car park, finding pictures of cars in magazines and making up a story involving a car, which was scribed for him by an adult and then acted out by a group at the end of the day (see story scribing in Chapter 4: December).

PSE teaching

The time spent on PSE is still considerable and numerous examples of this teaching appear on the planning sheets. Here are some examples:

Group arguing over the glider bike. 'I pointed out the timer and explained how it could be used for turn-taking. The group carried on playing, swopping the rider whenever the timer finished.

Group playing on PE apparatus and pushing each other. 'I explained that the rule when climbing anywhere is that 'you must not touch anyone'. The adult stayed near the group and gave a few more reminders before the group continued climbing without pushing.

Children playing in mud kitchen and getting mud on their clothes. 'I reminded them that they need to wear aprons. Children were not able to put the aprons on independently. 'I modelled how they could ask each other for help. The children helped each other put on the aprons and carried on playing.

Soo drew on Amy's picture. 'I modelled language and then Amy said to Soo 'Don't do that! I don't like it!'. The girls carried on drawing together and laughing.

October ends with an exhausted group of staff and a happy group of children. Routines, boundaries and expectations continue to be enforced so that children feel safe and confident. Staff are able to spend longer periods in meaningful interactions with individuals and groups because the majority of children are independent and involved in their learning. The half-term break is very welcome – a chance to rest and be ready for the next half-term.

3 November

This month brought some unexpected visitors to Carterhatch – OFSTED inspectors! The entry data (discussed in Chapter 2: October) was very useful and I describe the inspection and the outcome later in this chapter. I also describe how we cope with the challenges of the wet and windy weather. The individual folders that we have for each child are explained too. In the environment section I look at the water activities on offer indoors and outside. I also discuss maths provision and explain why we don't have a maths area. In the diary section, I have picked a few of the numerous examples of maths learning that happen amid the play everywhere and every day in the nursery.

NOVEMBER: TO DO LIST
- Re-establish routines, boundaries and expectations after half-term break.
- Continue with first round of focus children.
- Continue with first round of parent meetings.
- Review environment and resources.

Cold and wet!

November is one of the hardest months in the academic year. It is one of the few months without any holiday break or even any bank holidays. The weather is often wet and cold, making outdoor learning challenging because it is hard to keep the children warm, dry and relatively mud free! There is a constant stream of children changing into and out of coats, rainwear and wellington boots. When I was a foster carer three brothers came to live with me. They had devised their own method for getting their coats on independently and we now use this method in nursery. The coat is placed on the floor, or on a table, open and upside down. The child puts their arms in the sleeves and lifts the coat over their head! The fine motor control needed to do up a zip is also developed during these cold months.

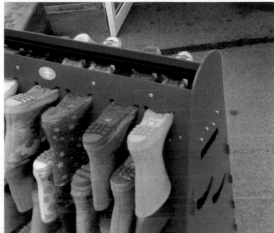

Wellington boots are stored on the Welly Wagon, which can be left outside since the boots are upside down!

Carterhatch Infant School has a wonderful outdoor play policy, which is shared with parents at the home visit (see Figure 3.1).

It is useful to have a document like this that parents can be referred to at various times during the year. We also ask that children have a spare set of clothes on their peg so that they can get changed if they get too wet. In the colder weather it is often a few staff members who are reluctant to go outside – the children run around and keep warm, very rarely complaining. It is essential that the adults' reluctance does not prevent the children going outside during the winter months. It is also essential to keep the doors open so that the children realise that the outdoor environment is still available. Plastic strips in the doorways help prevent the cold air getting indoors, while allowing the doors to be left open all day.

Policy on Outdoor Play

All children will be given the opportunity to play outside throughout most of the day whatever the weather.

It is important that you dress your child for school appropriately: warm clothes and waterproof coat when it's cold and wet; sun hat and sun screen when it's sunny.

Children get wet, muddy and messy when they play outside. We provide protective clothing for them to wear, including wellington boots, although you can provide these things for your child if you wish.

We teach children how to minimise how messy they get and they do get better at this as they get older, but it's part of their learning and development – you can't expect them not to get messed up playing in mud.

We will not compromise on allowing children to play outdoors as we believe it to be an essential component of young children's learning and development.

Children must be allowed to experience the world around them in a full, messy, muddy, wet environment if they are to make useful meaning of it.

P.S. Getting wet does not cause us to catch a cold. If the cold virus is around, we will pick it up regardless of whether we are wet or dry.

Figure 3.1 Carterhatch Infant School outdoor play policy

Individual folders

As mentioned, part of the preparations in nursery includes assembling a folder for each child. These are hard-backed A4 ring binders in various colours and they are stored in low units within the classroom so that the children can access them whenever they wish. Everything to do with the child is kept in their folder (except highly confidential information) as follows:

- *Information*: All the information gathered from the home visit is included, along with any reports or information from previous settings.
- *Special Book*: Each folder contains a 'Special Book' (some A3 sheets, folded and stapled into a book) and the children, parents and staff choose what to stick in this book. This booklet is taken to the home visit and, if they wish, the child can draw a picture on the front cover.

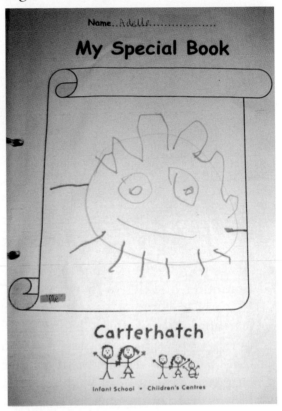

Items put into this booklet might include their stories, artwork, brochures from places they have visited, shopping lists etc. Some of the photos taken at home by the child with the school camera are also printed and stuck in here.

When the child talks about the photos, or other items in their book, an adult will scribe their comments next to the pictures. This is a simple and effective way of recording the child's voice. Each Special Book is unique to the individual child. If the book gets filled up, we can put another one into the folder. This is one advantage of a ring binder.

November 2013

'One day I went to the library. I get some books. I got one on peppa pig. I go back to nursery, back here. I cut the balloons. They fly away.' The end.

- *Nursery Profile*: One other main item in the folder is the child's 'Nursery Profile'. This is another booklet we have devised. This year it contains 17 sections – linked to the 17 early learning goals – and is used to store evidence (in the form of references to learning journeys [see Chapter 2: October for detailed explanation of learning journeys], observations, photos, final products, notes from parents etc.) relating to the child's level of development in that particular area. The observations are not long narrative observations – our learning journeys have replaced the need for these. However, they do include 'snapshot' observations of the children, particularly when they do something independently or for the first time. We call these 'Wow!' moments. For example 'Jayden went to the toilet on his own and remembered to wash his hands'. Or 'Sasha said "Help me please!" in a loud clear voice'. These observations might be accompanied by a photo and will be dated and annotated to explain why they are noteworthy for a particular child. The two photos below show pages from two profile booklets. Jacqui has opted to highlight the sections at the top, but there is no obligation to do this – the judgements of levels are supposed to be a 'best fit' approach. However, with 60 children to assess, it is difficult to hold every bit of information in your head.

As stated, there is no statutory requirement to use any particular document for tracking progress through nursery. We, like many settings, have taken the easy option and use *Development Matters* as a guide. As the guidance recommends we take a 'best fit' approach. On entry and then at the end of each half term, we assess which developmental band best describes the child. The computer package that the school is using requires an assessment of whether the child is 'entering', 'working within' or 'secure' in any particular band. Although this is a very tedious and time-consuming exercise, it does provide a detailed picture of the progress that each child is making. It also highlights any areas where progress is not apparent – either for an individual or for

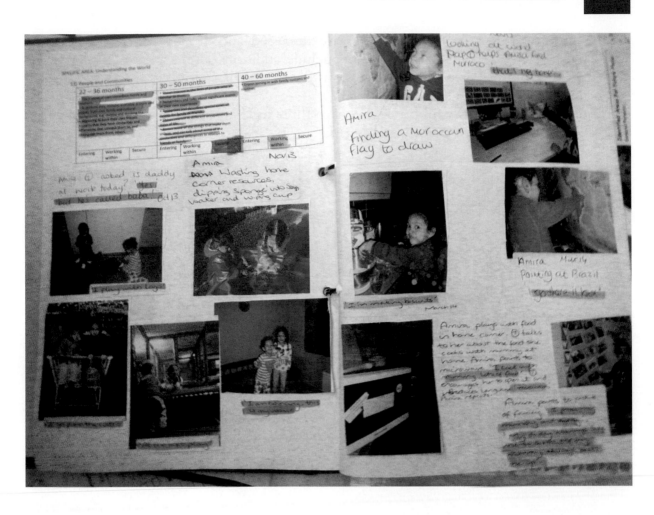

the group as a whole. Such findings are discussed and, if deemed necessary, then changes can be made. Changes might include additions/alterations to the environment, the routines or possibly the sessions for a particular child. Progress is discussed in more detail in the Chapter 5: January.

- *Learning journeys*: Each child will also have three learning journeys in their folder by the end of the year; one from each term.

Many settings are opting for purely electronic record keeping. In nursery there are always children looking at their folders and talking to each other and staff about their learning. These valuable interactions would be lost if we had no 'paper' records, printed photos and folders.

A time-saving tip

Every day there are numerous photos and 'snap-shot' observations taken about the children ('Wow' moments). I have visited many settings to find a collection like this:

£10 buys a box file with a suspension file for each of the 30 children in a class. Photos, notes, children's work and observations can be dropped into the corresponding compartment instantly. Teachers spend their planning and preparation (PPA) time updating pupil folders but they do not need to waste any time sorting through a mountain of papers – they just lift out the suspension file for a particular child and everything is to hand. This has saved staff hours!

Key workers

It is a legal requirement for each child to have a key worker, but there is no stipulation about how a setting organises this. For the younger children in our children's centres, it is vital that they have a familiar key worker to whom they can form an attachment. Indeed, advances in the understanding of attachment theory and attachment disorders underpin this piece of legislation. In brief, a baby, who receives responsive care and attention from their main carer, will develop a good attachment and relationship to that carer. As they grow older, they will be able to form successful relationships with others. Conversely if a baby receives inadequate or inconsistent care and attention they can develop an attachment disorder, and one of the main outcomes of this is an inability to form relationships as they grow older.

Obviously for a young baby in day care from 8 am till 6 pm, the practitioner is their main carer and this needs to be the same person for as much of that time as possible. However, in nursery and reception, most children will have developed a strong attachment to a parent and are able to cope with shared attention from a few adults in nursery. We therefore say that the teacher will be the key worker for all the children, supported by the other members of staff. If a child or parent forms a trusting working relationship with a particular member of the staff team, then they can always chat to them. Also, the support staff help with updating folders, making observations and taking photos. However, it is ultimately the teacher's responsibility to maintain the paperwork and to take ownership of the class and the progress of *all* the children.

OFSTED

The OFSTED inspection happened on my birthday! The phone call came on Tuesday lunchtime and then the inspectors were in school Wednesday and Thursday. This is the fourth inspection I have been through in the past six years and in each case the Foundation Stage has been graded as 'Outstanding'. Inspectors want to give an accurate grade but it is up to the setting to provide them with the evidence. I have therefore learnt how to make sure that a setting is recognised for what it is achieving and how to ensure it is graded correctly. Of course that means that the setting must be operating in the best possible way, achieving outstanding progress while maintaining the excellent child-led approach that I am advocating. Once this is established then we, as practitioners, need to be proactive and passionate in our approach to an inspection.

Foundation Stage team leaders or someone from the Senior Leadership Team (SLT) have important tasks to complete in preparation for an inspection:

- Prepare a self-evaluation, including as much evidence as you can (we use a document called 'Quality Matters' – which can be downloaded at www.freedomtolearn.co.uk/links).
- Keep a copy of your 'Teaching and Learning Policy' to give the inspectors. Make sure this includes an explanation of your rationale.
- Make sure your data are always up to date and that you understand them (the present year and the previous year's data will be needed).
- Download the latest OFSTED inspector's handbook and the level descriptors – if you know what evidence they need, then you can point them in the right direction.
- Don't avoid the inspectors – seek them out and talk to them – explain how your setting is organised and why – be knowledgeable and confident that you are doing the best for the children.
- Accompany the inspectors as much as possible and point out what is important, explain the background of individual children, talk about things you have changed and are planning to change.
- Once you get the call, gather all information relating to three children to use as 'case studies' to discuss with the inspectors.
- Ask them what other information they need and be prepared to go and find it.

Inspectors might ask to see the plan for the day. If you have read Chapter 2: October, you will realise that **we do not do any written forward planning**. Obviously when I tell the inspectors that we don't have any plans then a dialogue begins. This is the perfect opportunity to explain how we work (in the moment), and why (because it leads to deep-level learning), and to offer to escort them around the setting to see exactly what we mean. This is what I have done during each of the past four inspections.

You need to show that the **children are making good or outstanding progress over time** (with summarised data and examples of evidence). During the inspection you need to show that the **children are displaying high levels of involvement** (see Introduction) and **making progress within a short space of time**.

Inspectors are used to judging levels of engagement, independence, confidence, creativity etc. This is exactly the same as levels of involvement. Point out high levels of involvement and also examples of progress happening during the inspection. For example during this inspection a child was trying, and failing, to cut a piece of paper because the scissors were held awkwardly. The adult corrected the grip and the child cut the paper easily.

Another example was a child drawing a dinosaur and they didn't know what the teeth would look like. An adult helped them look on the iPad and found pictures of dinosaur teeth so that they could complete the drawing accurately. There were examples of progress happening at every moment. This is the most important aspect of child-led learning – opportunities for teaching are grasped and exploited immediately – therefore progress is rapid.

These children were picking up stones and arguing as to who had more. Jacqui grasped this teachable moment and used it to demonstrate how to count large groups of objects. The children soon realised that it was difficult to count the stones in Jacqui's hands, but once they were lined up on the floor they were able to make the comparison easily.

During this inspection, I spent well over six hours with the inspectors, escorting them around the setting for over three hours, carrying out joint formal observations for an hour (and then being observed myself as I fed back to the teachers) and being interviewed for nearly two hours. I had everything ready as indicated on the list above and the interview centred around these documents. I also gave them a copy of Ferre Laevers' (1994) 'Levels of Involvement' (see Appendix 1) and explained how much we use these levels to assess classes and individuals. Inspectors will check that what you claim matches up with what they observe during the inspection, what they see in the children's folders and what the data show. This inspection concluded with the best possible result for the school – an overall grade of 'Outstanding'. Some of the comments relating to the early years were wonderful:

> *All children make an exceptional start to their education because of excellent provision in the Early Years Foundation Stage … very high quality independent learning by children from the time they enter nursery … the outside area is used exceptionally well to encourage children's independent investigative skills and their physical development … children explore confidently and show curiosity in all that is around them …* [and my favourite bit] ***In the EYFS all learning takes place at the behest of the children and adults follow them***.

Many practitioners are worried that OFSTED expect to see detailed plans and formal teaching. That is not the case. Their own guidance states 'Inspectors must not expect teaching staff to teach in any specific way. Schools and teachers should decide for themselves how to teach so that children are engaged in lessons, acquire knowledge and learn well'. OFSTED does not prescribe any particular sort of planning or teaching. It is interested in the impact that a setting is having. Prove to the inspectors that you are achieving outstanding progress with happy, independent, engaged children and you will not be challenged about your planning or about a child-led approach.

Setting up the environment

Water

Water fascinates young children and it is a vital component of any early years setting. Indoors, the water play is limited by the need to avoid flooding the whole class! The water tray is filled every day in nursery but the resources are left on the shelf nearby for the children to select independently.

I often use the phrase 'less is more' when giving advice about environments. It is easy to have 20 boats, when actually 3 boats of varying sizes is sufficient. As with any area, we monitor the levels of involvement to assess whether it is working. As with the indoor sand area, the bottom shelf contains trays, the

contents of which can be changed if levels of involvement drop. The higher shelves are shadowed and this makes tidying up a game in itself.

Outside, we have again used shopping baskets to store resources – with the baskets attached to the fence with cup hooks. This means that there is no need to set up the water area – the resources are left in place, ready to be used. They include buckets, jugs, funnels, pipes, brushes, sponges, bottles, boats, water animals etc. Attached to the fence are some fishing nets. Nearby are two Funky Fountains and a Creative Cascade set. One of the two water trays has pulleys attached and both are filled every day. The children are also able to collect their own water from the water butt. Water is transported to water plants, wet the sand, mix with mud, pour down the Cascade pipes, fill saucepans … and anything else the children think of.

Setting up the environment

Maths

We do not have a maths area. This is a deliberate decision. Young children do not see maths (or any other subject) as distinct or separate from the everyday business of their play and exploration. It is just another aspect to their play and occurs in every area of the nursery. Figure 3.2 gives some examples of maths opportunities and demonstrates how absurd it is to try and keep maths to just one area of the class or garden. I have not specified it in Figure 3.2, but there are many sets of numicon shapes around the nursery – in the playdough, the sand, the water, the mud kitchen, the role play area, small construction area and displayed on the walls.

Area	Mathematical opportunities
Outdoor PE equipment area (chalk board attached to wall nearby)	Different size balls. Keeping count or score and comparing. Comparing/measuring distances jumped or distances travelled by a ball etc. Ordinal numbers. Positional language.
Large- and small-scale construction – including beads, cars, Lego, animals etc.	Measurements of structures built. Shape, size and number of blocks (or other construction toys) used. Properties of various shapes. Positional language. Sorting and classifying cars, animals, etc. Creating patterns – symmetrical and repeating, sorting and ordering by size, colour, shape with beads, cars etc.
Mud kitchen Water areas Sand areas Playdough Cooking	Capacity and associated language. Counting when creating/following recipes. Comparing size and shape of containers and cutters. Creating patterns with stones, leaves, sticks, shells, candles etc. Catching and counting fish etc. Using balance and associated language. Matching shapes to shadows on shelves to tidy up.
Digging area	Counting legs on insects. Comparing length and thickness of worms. Language of size when digging holes.
Wheeled toys	Numicon and numeral attached for matching and numeral recognition in associated parking bays. Use of timer for turn-taking. Discussion and comparison of speed. Counting and comparison of wheels.
Music area	Bells ordered and numbered. Operating compact disk player – selecting numbered tracks. Counting beats on drum etc. Creating patterns with sound.
Den building	Size, shape, height discussions. Counting pegs used/needed. Discussion about capacity of den built.
Woodwork	Size, shape and related properties of various pieces of wood. Counting numbers of wheels, strings, windows etc. needed for train, bike, guitar etc. Understanding of weight of various pieces of wood and tools. Use of positional language.

Role play	Use of clocks, telephones, cookers, remote controls, money, balance, scales, recipe books, sets of plates and cutlery etc., leading to discussion, experience and understanding of concepts associated with shape, space, measure and number.
Creative area	Shapes, size, number in creations – with boxes, collage etc. Creating patterns. Sewing – size, shape of fabric and thread.
Self-register and visual timetable	Counting and comparing numbers of children. Developing language and concepts of time and ordering of events.
Interactive whiteboard, Ipads	Various computer games available for every aspect of the maths curriculum.
Books, puzzles, games	Available in carpet areas and outdoor investigation and reading area and include topics such as shape, number, colour, time, size etc.
Snack area	Shape, size of fruit. Capacity concepts with drinks. Fractions: half, quarter, etc.

Figure 3.2 Maths opportunities and where they take place

Clearly we have equipment available in all areas and this is described in more detail in each particular area in other chapters of the book.

A word of warning: be very careful in the use of questions when interacting with young children. It is easy to spoil a meaningful experience with an inappropriate question. For example if a child is enacting a magical tale with a flying horse and a princess, then don't ask how many legs are on the horse! You may laugh, but that is exactly what I witnessed when visiting a nursery last month. The child looked up at the adult, put the horse back in the tray and went outside. Smart move!

Diary extracts: Examples of mathematical aspects to play

WHAT TO LOOK OUT FOR
- Children settle back into nursery routines quickly after the half term break.
- The environment is meeting the needs of the children so levels of involvement are high.
- Staff are able to engage in longer interactions with individuals and groups.
- Children have formed firm friendship groups.
- Maths is happening everywhere at various levels.

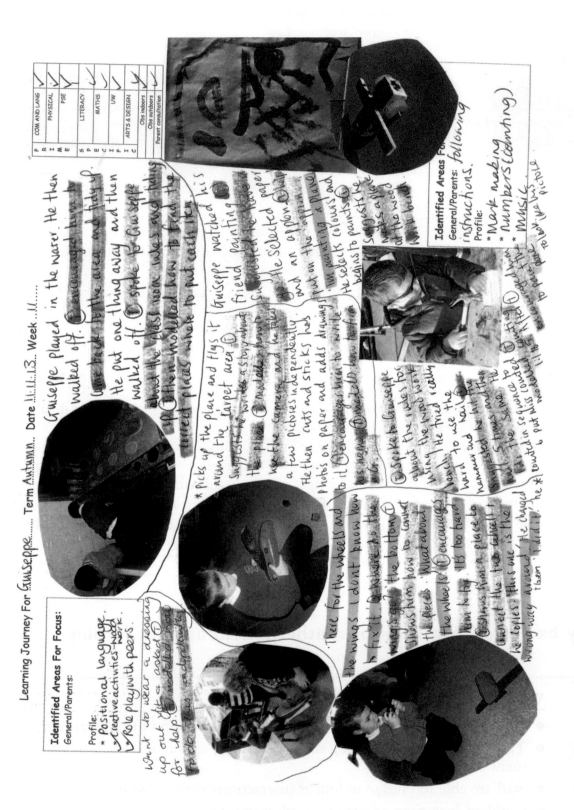

Figure 3.3 Sample learning journey for November

Note: See Chapter 2: October for explanation.

As usual it is challenging to select events to include in the diary – there is so much happening every day. However, this month I have picked out some examples of the maths activities that the children have initiated, including some that have been pursued independently and others that have been supported and extended through the skilled interactions of the staff.

Number

Alex made a train at the woodwork bench. He used a brio train to look at and check how many wheels he needed.

Osuani found the numicon shapes in the garden and spontaneously started to line them up in order. He displayed high-level involvement and clearly enjoyed the feel of the shapes and the challenge of ordering them.

By having the numicon shapes available in all areas of the nursery, they are used by all children, whatever area they prefer to play in. The adults can respond to such events, observing, assessing and challenging if appropriate for a particular child.

Saja was delighted to search and find a piece of numicon to match her age. She pointed to the number and to herself, smiling.

Edona persevered to produce this collection of hearts. As she made each one, she counted the line again – seeing and feeling the concept of 'one more' as she played.

The concept of 'one more' was experienced in the context of the woodwork bench when Aleyna made this birthday cake. She was determined that there would be ten candles and in this case she was able to say the next number without counting from the beginning each time. The spot of orange paint for the candle flames was a lovely touch.

The concept of 'one less' is equally challenging to verbalise but Malachi demonstrated a clear understanding during his game as he sang '7 fat sausages sizzling in the pan!'.

Zipporah asked when her Mum was coming to collect her. Jacqui pointed out the visual timetable and the clocks near the door. She explained that when the clock hand reached number three, then it would be tidy up time. She then said that Michael (the puppet) also wanted to know when his Mum was coming and that maybe Zipporah could make him a watch to help him understand. The watch-making distracted Zipporah and she became deeply involved in the activity.

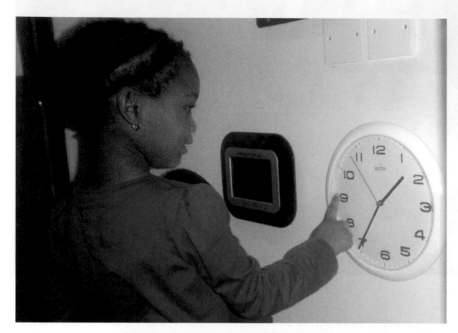

The staff in the nursery know each child very well. In this case, Jacqui knew that Zipporah was able to recognise numerals and also that she had excellent pencil control. It was therefore appropriate to suggest the challenge of the watch-making activity.

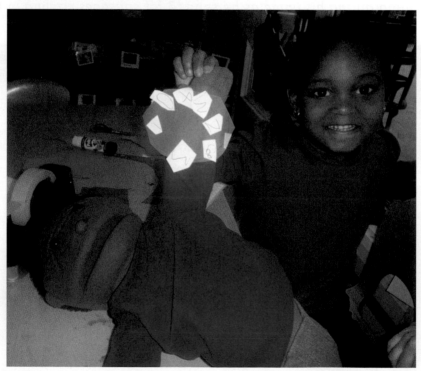

This group of children started playing with the Creative Cascade set – rolling balls down the pipes. They watched the balls roll away and then ran to collect them. Jacqui joined the group and encouraged them to use chalk to mark where the balls rolled to. This led to the development of vocabulary associated with distance. Jacqui then extended the activity by suggesting they try the pipe at different heights on the Cascade stand and again comparing distances that the balls travel.

A simple game led to the development of mathematical vocabulary and concepts associated with distance and height.

The children have had several opportunities to make cakes now (see Chapter 7: March) and the skills they have developed during that activity are now being applied in other situations. This group pretended that the playdough was butter. They discussed the balance, using language associated with weight and also demonstrated a grasp of the concepts.

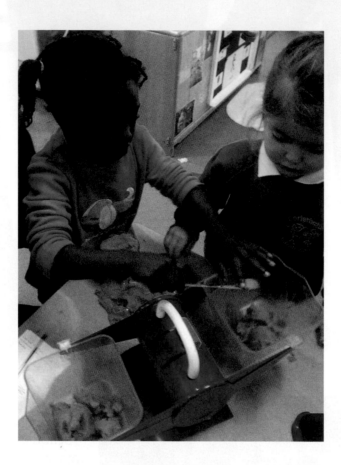

A group of children were playing independently with the set of log slices. Initially they made a long line of single logs and walked along them. They then rearranged the logs into piles of three. They then walked carefully along this, much shorter line, of steps.

30 divided by 1 = 30

30 divided by 3 = 10

Or

1 X 30 = 30

3 X 10 = 30

Is division and multiplication on the nursery curriculum? It was on this day!

It is a common **misconception** that children have to verbalise a concept before we can be sure that they understand it. They do need to experience it again and again in various contexts and we need to observe them carefully to see if they transfer the knowledge. We don't need to ask them lots of questions. In this case the children realised that the higher the piles of logs, the shorter the path would be. But they may not have been able to explain that in words. Similarly we see Baran performing a complex maths investigation with the cars as shown here.

1 X 20 = 20
2 X 10 = 20

Michael's photos from home showed that he had pet snakes. This interest was built upon during Michael's focus week. At the creative table he made a two-dimensional model with coloured paper. With support and encouragement from the staff, he was able to make a more realistic model by sewing and creating a three-dimensional snake. Later in the week, Michael brought in a snake skin that stretched almost the width of the carpet area. Throughout the week, the staff were using mathematical vocabulary and the children were having mathematical experiences.

Other children were fascinated by the snakes and Rayhan can be seen here acting out a story that he wrote (see Chapter 4: December for details of story scribing and acting).

The revised EYFS states:

> **Mathematics** involves providing children with opportunities to develop and improve their skills in counting, understanding and using numbers, calculating simple addition and subtraction problems; and to describe shapes, spaces, and measures.
>
> (DfES 2014: 8)

It is clear from this one month alone that the nursery is providing just such opportunities in abundance. The huge variety of languages spoken by the children means that we may not be able to assess them all verbally. Also, as stated earlier, sometimes young children grasp concepts even if they do not have the language to explain them. However, the staff can see the maths happening, provide accurate vocabulary and commentary and give suggestions to extend the learning when appropriate. The OFSTED inspectors recognised this and acknowledged the skilled interactions that they observed. They also noticed how staff did not always intervene and how important it was to let the children persevere with a task in order to find a solution for themselves.

As November came to an end, the staff were delighted that their efforts were acknowledged in the 'Outstanding' grade from OFSTED. It gave them a well-needed boost to get through the few weeks of December to the end of the long autumn term.

4 December

It is almost impossible to ignore Christmas if you are living in England and many of the children at nursery celebrate Christmas at home. In this chapter I discuss our approach to such events. I also describe how we use carpet (or group) sessions, explain story scribing and look at the data for the first term. In the environment section I describe some of the opportunities for literacy activities that are in almost all areas of the nursery, and look at the role play provision. In the diary section I have picked out a few occasions when the play and exploration in the nursery led into literacy activities.

DECEMBER: TO DO LIST

- Complete first cycle of focus children.
- Complete first cycle of parent meetings.
- Update individual folders.
- Introduce story scribing and acting.
- Update assessments and data summaries.
- Review provision in response to assessments (if necessary).
- Organise end of term party (if you wish).
- Discuss religious festivals with team and decide how to proceed.

Christmas

As with everything else, we take our lead from the children with regard to the introduction of Christmas. However, it is up to the adults to decide how to develop the inevitable interest and excitement.

Krys took this photo at home when he was a focus child. Many other children were keen to talk about their Christmas trees too when they saw this picture.

This year several of the focus children had photos of a Christmas tree at home. Harley was particularly animated talking about her tree and the decorations. The staff agreed that they would like to put up a tree in class. With the discovery that there were hardly any decorations, the children set about making their own!

Eren sets about making his own tree decoration.

Many of the photos from home reflect religious or traditional events. In many cases the children are simply aware that they wore special clothes or that they had a special meal. What is important in nursery is that all the children feel comfortable about sharing their experiences. Any setting develops its own 'culture' in this way because it is made up of many unique children, each with unique life experiences. One of the most important things we can do as practitioners is to develop within the group a culture of respect, acceptance, interest and enjoyment of the diversity. We do not, therefore, become stressed and anxious trying to make sure that we mention and celebrate every cultural event during the year. The details and facts about each child's culture are important to them – the atmosphere in which they are received in nursery is important to everyone.

Group sessions

At the end of the morning and afternoon there is a group session. This is the only time the children are interrupted in their exploration and play. The children tidy up and gather on the carpet. We again use the levels of involvement to assess whether these sessions are appropriate. For example if a story is being read and the children appear as they do in the photo below, then clearly the story, or the way it is being delivered, is appropriate.

Some of the individual folders can be seen behind these girls. They are stored in low units so that the children can access them whenever they wish.

However, if the group is not engaged, then it is not that the children are doing anything wrong, rather we are not meeting their needs. It is often easier to maintain high levels of involvement with a smaller group, when you can 'pitch' the activity to meet more of their needs and interests. Therefore we try, whenever possible, to split the group into two or three small groups.

When children opt to go and listen to a story during session time, then the level of involvement is often higher than at the end of a session when they are tired and waiting to go home.

These sessions are used for singing, story reading, showing things that children have made, talking about things the children have been doing or explaining about new or different equipment or events. Many of these activities involve aspects of phase one phonics and we use cued articulation whenever we wish the children to focus on a particular sound. For example, Jacqui might ask all children who have the sound 'a' at the start of their name to stand up. When she says the sound 'a', she will accompany it with the associated cue, as used by speech therapists. This system is continued in reception and the nursery children will already be familiar with the sound and the cue. Some nursery children will also be associating the sound with the letter as well, but this is not a priority for nursery – confidence working within phase one is our aim for this year group. One other activity that occurs regularly at group time is story acting as described below. These sessions are also used to show some of the photos that the children have taken at home.

Story scribing and acting

By December the children are confident in the environment and many are creating wonderful models and pictures as well as developing story lines within their role play. Whenever the staff feel it is appropriate, they will offer to scribe a story for a child. For example when Maria made this castle, Jacqui approached her and said 'I wonder what you have made!'. The use of the phrase 'I wonder …' is a great way to elicit a response from any child. It is a statement, rather than a question, and does not necessarily require a response. Therefore, it is not at all threatening and the child invariably responds.

Maria is delighted with her model and keen to 'write' a story about it to be shared with the class at the end of the session.

In this example, Jacqui then offered to scribe Maria's story about the castle. When writing the story, it is important for the child to watch the adult write and for the adult to write exactly what the child says. In this way, even the youngest child learns that their spoken words can be transferred onto paper. They also see how writing is formed and what it looks like. The exact words that the child says are written down, even if grammatically incorrect (see Appendix D for adult prompt sheet).

As the year progresses and the children create more stories, then these transcripts become a record of the child's language development. For some children it will be appropriate to suggest that they add their name at the end of the story. As the year progresses, there might be a few children in the nursery who are able and keen to write a few other letters or words within their story.

Maria has collected her name card to copy – ensuring everyone knows that she is the author of the story.

At the end of the session (morning or afternoon), the stories are shown to the group and an adult selects some children to act as the characters in the story. Then the story is read aloud and the children 'act' the story. When this activity is first introduced, and the children see a story being acted out, then many more of them will be keen to write a story the next day.

The stories are kept in the children's folders and become a record of their language development, their story-writing development, their imagination, sometimes their understanding of the world (depending on the content of the story) and sometimes their pencil control (if there is a picture or if they have added their name).

For example the following stories (and many others) appear in one child's folder:

- *November*: 'I am butterfly. I fly. I go home'. The end.
- *January*: 'I am a butterfly and I always fly. I fly to little Africa and you have to play there. And then we finished. We go back to our home'. The end.
- *March*: 'One day there was a little, little butterfly. He fly to little toy's house. Then he hop in the car and drive away to Africa. When he is finished in Africa he fly back home. Then there were two little fairies. They find a flying pony and fly all the way to the moon. Then when it's finished they fly back home'. The end.
- *May*: 'One night a flying boat with magic sleeped and woke up, had lunch. He went in the forest. Then he fly into the down, down, down, down and goes deeped where the forest is. He found the very mean dragon and killed it, he was evil. He used the magical thing to kill it. And he fly back home and had the milk'. The end.

- *July*: 'There was a big, big tiger. He was friendly and there was a friendly bat and a friendly bear. They found some friends to play with. They flied through the forest and to the moon. They lived there. Then they found a rainbow and flied to the end of it and found a treasure and went back home'. The end.

On this occasion, Jacqui is reading the story and Melissa is giving acting tips to the children!

In recent years there has been a lot of concern and debate about the apparent low attainment of boys in the early learning goal of 'writing'. Teachers have been put under a lot of pressure to 'improve' attainment in this area. Inevitably, this pressure has been transferred to the children. Last month, when I was visiting another school, a four-year-old boy said to me 'I am no good at writing'. What are we doing to these children? A four year old should feel that they can achieve anything and they should feel supremely confident and able to tackle every challenge they face.

In the nursery and reception classes in our school **we never tell the children to write**. I repeat – **we never tell the children to write**. We wait until they show an interest in writing something and then we 'pounce' – we capture that moment of interest and motivation to develop this area of learning. For the majority of children in nursery, this will entail mark-making or watching an adult write. In reception that moment of interest in writing might well occur when the child is able to do some of the writing themselves. With the 'top-down' pressure in schools, it is easy to become anxious and to try and 'force' the writing but experience has shown that the wait is worthwhile. Story scribing is a fantastic way to motivate children to want to write. It is also a great way to teach them about the process of writing well before they may be physically able to do any writing themselves. Starting formal teaching of writing at an earlier age does **not** lead to higher academic attainment at a later age. Indeed putting pressure on young children to read and write before they are developmentally ready and before they are interested can have the opposite effect – it can put them off literacy activities for life. We aim to do the reverse – they become so fascinated and excited about what can be achieved by reading and writing that they are nagging us to have a go – **never us nagging them**!!

Data at the end of term

As explained in Chapter 3: November, OFSTED need to assess the progress of the children, but they do not specify a particular method for data collection or tracking. A brief summary is the best starting point and more detail can be supplied if particular issues arise. It is possible to complete an inspection without supplying any numerical data – rather the 'journey' of each child can be explained. However, OFSTED will still report in terms of 'proportions' of children. In our case we gave the inspectors a grid like the one below and they were satisfied. This grid shows percentages in each group for 'on entry' and 'term one'. Extra rows will be added each term.

Nursery	% well below expected level	% below expected level	% at expected level	% above expected level
Entry September 2013	37	43	15	5
Term 1 December 2013	22	42	31	5

Figure 4.1 Term 1 progress data for OFSTED

The progress of the whole cohort is clear. However, this is meaningless in terms of helping us make decisions about the provision or about individual children. The folders for each child provide rich and detailed information about the journeys they have travelled. Through discussions, we decide if any particular child is causing concern and if there is anything extra we should be doing. By looking at the collated data, we can see if there is a lack of progress in any particular areas of development for the cohort as a whole. This might indicate the need to amend the timetable or the provision. This term, the data confirmed that all children were making progress in line with, or ahead of our expectations of them as individuals. A few children had made limited progress, but in every case we knew exactly what the story of that child was and why their progress was as it was. It did not come as a surprise.

Setting up the environment

Literacy opportunities

Reading and writing are not an end in themselves — they are a means to an end. This vital point is being ignored in many schools where children are being forced to read and write at younger and younger ages, purely for the sake of passing a test. No wonder they don't like writing very much. No wonder they don't opt to write when they are able to choose what to do. The children at Carterhatch write for various reasons: to remember what to buy at the shop, to remember what to put in the cake, to create a wonderful story that will be read to the class, to send a message to their mum or a friend, to ask the site staff to do a job, to ask the head teacher for a new resource, to give instructions about something, to keep the scores in a game, to make sure everyone knows who a masterpiece belongs to, to know which fruit and vegetables are growing etc. Thus they write shopping lists, recipes, stories, letters, notices, score sheets, labels etc. No wonder, then, that there are always children writing in our nursery and reception classes.

The resources to support 'writing' are in several areas of the nursery and there are also clip boards so that the children can take paper and pens etc. to any areas they wish. We don't have a 'writing area' because, as seen above, young children do not see writing as something separate to their normal activity – it is just another part of their play. However, the resources are always to hand, clearly labelled, well stocked and with a wide variety of mark making implements, paper, notebooks and card. Indoors the main stock is in the creative area and outdoors there is a trolley with similar resources. Outside there are also chalks as well as large decorating brushes and rollers for mark-making with water on the ground and walls.

It is simple to make your own outdoor blackboard – buy a piece of marine ply wood and paint it with blackboard paint.

For a young child the most significant piece of literacy is their name. We have name cards, which also have photos on them and these are attached to a unit with Velcro. The children are able to find their own name or those of their friends if they want to label work or write a letter etc.

We are lucky that we have an area that is sheltered in the garden and this unit can be left outside. However, a unit such as this one (from Community Playthings) is easy to wheel in and out of a storage shed if you don't have a shelter or it can be covered with a tarpaulin at night or in the rain.

Similarly reading is not confined to one area of the nursery or garden. Information books are available in the creative areas (to give information on how to make things), near the guinea pigs (with information on how to care for the animals) and on the investigation unit (so that children can look up information about the creatures that they find or about plants that are growing). There are cookery books in the home corner and in the cooking area. Fiction books are available on both carpet areas as well as outdoors. The sofa indoors and cushions outdoors create comfortable areas in which stories can be shared. The diary section gives a few examples of how the resources have been used recently.

Setting up the environment

Role play

Real cans of food have been included in the home corner. Try to find cans without pull tabs – we have found a child eating the baked beans before.

If you ask children in Key Stage 2 or even Key Stage 3 what it is they remember about nursery, many of them will say 'the home corner!'. They have strong and fond memories of the 'miniature' house and the serious play that went on there. It is a vital component of young children's play as they take on the roles of the adults that they see around them. They put themselves into the position of someone else, imagine what that person would say, feel and do, and then act accordingly. This is a powerful way to develop empathy, which is defined as 'Identification with and understanding of another's situation, feelings, and motives'. It is tempting for adults to create complex role play areas but the home corner is the most familiar and therefore

most relevant to nursery children. Other interests arise during the year and there is a small area that is used to create a 'pop-up' doctors, vets, shop etc. But the house is kept permanently – both indoors and outside. As with all areas, we try to organise the area so that the children can tidy it easily. Therefore, particularly indoors, we limit the amount of resources. So there are two dolls (not 22!) and there are four cups etc.

Again we use the levels of involvement to determine whether we have got the provision right – too many resources and the children can't organise them to play purposefully, too few resources and the children might not have enough to do. In either case the levels of involvement will be low. When the resources are appropriate – in the amount, variety and complexity, then involvement will be high. Indoors, the resources tend to be more realistic, but children will use anything to maintain the play, so a piece of numicon will become a biscuit or a wooden block will be a mobile phone.

This photo shows the outdoor role play area. At the top of the photo you can see a salt bin – a fantastic storage solution. In this one we keep dolls, cushions and other resources that need protection from the rain.

Outdoors the sand, woodchip, mud and grass are the best possible cooking ingredients.

Diary extracts: Examples of literacy aspects to play

WHAT TO LOOK OUT FOR

- End of term data shows outstanding progress.
- Many children begin to experiment with mark–making.
- Many children become highly aware of text in the environment.
- The confidence levels of the children are very high.
- The children are more willing to take risks.
- Over-excitement and exhaustion can affect some children at the end of this long term.

So much happened in December and the inevitable excitement about Christmas did creep into the nursery as explained earlier in this chapter. It was also noticeable how so many children became very aware of text and writing possibilities. I have again selected just a few events to describe here.

Literacy

December was wet, wet, wet and these children enjoyed helping to clear some of the puddles. Literacy??? There is a saying 'If you can't say it, you can't write it'. Spoken language is a vital prerequisite for reading and writing. Melissa was having a conversation with these children as they worked – providing the new vocabulary if necessary, discussing where the puddle had come from, wondering where they could push the water to etc. The scope of the conversation was wide. Puddles, brooms, evaporation and flooding might well appear in the stories these children write in years to come. In addition they

Learning Journey For Malachi M.. Term Autumn.... Date 9/12/13. Week 15.....

Entries should include the initial observation (and assessment), the teaching and the outcome.

Identified Areas For Focus:
General/Parents:
Speech (parent concern)
Profile:
* Count → 5
* Extend vocabulary
*

Malachi walking around with a basket filled with cakes and pizza. (T) asked if he had some pizza to share. He took them out and counted 1:1 to four (T) using modelled words to say 'pizza using tricount at playdough (missed 5 Sam)

Malachi climbing on climbing frame with hat in his hand.

Malachi counts 1,2,3 with (T) and then jumps.

Malachi on the phone in the home corner. (T) asked who he was talking to. 'My mum' 'where is your mum?' 'At home' 'Wheres our?' (T) Malachi using sign, attention. The in and Malachi repeated and said 'chair'. There is just their his outside. He carried it in avoiding obstacles. 'What's that?' (T) told him it was pasta he repeated. He then said ''cause me' to Olivia she ignored him so he said (T) to encourage him to say and telling to even would this away and he went on to do the washing up and press buttons on the phone.

Malachi asked to play the iPad. (T) gave him the iPad he was able to turn it on and select an app independently. He chose a matching game. (T) encouraged him to match. After several attempts he got the idea and went on to successfully match all the items in the puzzle.

Malachi struggles to make his phone.

Malachi does this with (T)'s support.

Identified Areas For Future Focus:
General/Parents:
Speech / assertiveness
Profile:
* Confidence climbing
* Count → 10
*

		✓
P	COM AND LANG	✓
R	PHYSICAL	✓
I		
M	PSE	✓
E		
S	LITERACY	✓
P	MATHS	✓
E		
C	UW	✓
I		
F	ARTS & DESIGN	✓
I	Obs indoors	✓
C	Obs outdoors	✓
	Parent consultation	✓

Figure 4.2 Sample learning journey for December

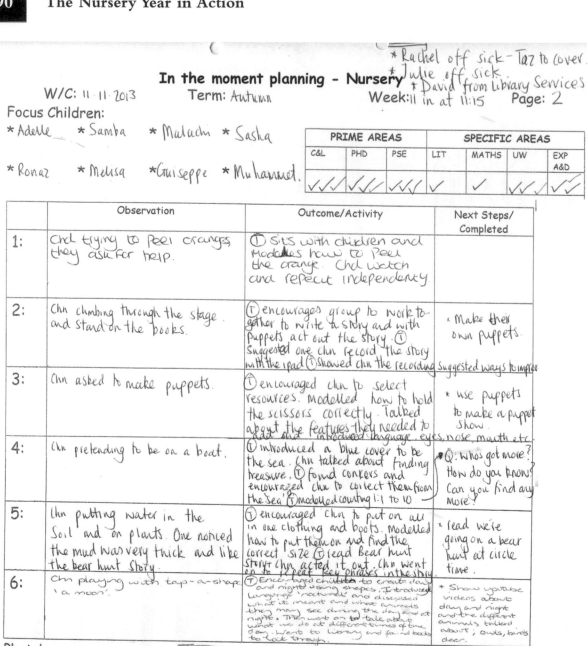

Photo's

Figure 4.3 Sample 'Planning in the moment' sheet

Note: See Chapter 2: October for explanation. There are eight focus children, six from the nursery and
two from the children's centre.

are developing their hand and arm muscles as well as their coordination. This physical development is another prerequisite for writing – the large motor skills need to be developed before the fine motor skills. Finally this was a new experience, something they had never done before and they were willing to have a go, take the risk and enjoy the challenge in an atmosphere where they knew their efforts would be recognised and supported. This disposition to learning is probably the most crucial to all development and will allow them to take risks and 'have a go' when it comes to reading and writing in future. Indeed reading and writing will be approached in the same way as this puddle – a new experience to be tackled, with the support of a caring adult – and in that atmosphere it will be enjoyed!

Lots of rescue games were being played in the garden and this baby became trapped at the top of a tower! There were lengthy discussions about how to rescue her and various attempts were made using ropes and sticks. Eventually one child asked for a ladder and the rescue was successful! Here again the prerequisites for reading and writing are all present – spoken language is developed and a narrative emerged; physical skills are developed – balancing on a ladder etc; and again we see the personal and social skills involved in developing an idea, having the confidence to make suggestions, being willing to take risks and experiencing the success.

As stated above, reference books are available in many areas of the nursery. These girls are using a book to get ideas for how to decorate their cakes. They will not need a literacy lesson about 'non-fiction' books and what they are for – they are already using them for the correct purpose.

The Christmas conversations continued and Santa was a main topic. Several children said they had 'written' to Santa with a Christmas list. Other children then wanted to do this too. Obviously this was a fantastic opportunity to 'pounce' on the desire to write. Staff supported children to draw pictures or stick on pictures of the toys that they wanted. Some children were able, and therefore encouraged, to add their name. Others watched as the adults scribed the wish list for them. The discussion then moved onto the address needed for Santa and finally there was a trip to the post box to send the letters on their way.

The Makaton that was introduced from day one in the nursery is now being used confidently by all children. Here we see Alara using the symbol cards and playing 'teacher' – encouraging her friends to join in the signing with her. She is actually 'reading' the cards – looking at the symbol, but also seeing the word on each card, and then producing the appropriate sign and saying the word. There are several sets of these cards and the children enjoy playing with them and practising their signing skills.

Many children in the nursery are becoming aware of letters and the associated sounds that they make. This comes about when they watch adults scribe, when they look at name cards, displays, books and folders. Many children are also attempting to write their own name and a few children are beginning to show an interest in writing other things too. I cannot stress enough how we treat each child as an individual and use levels of involvement to determine whether an activity is appropriate. When Kayra started to draw various objects, it was her idea. She drew an apple, a bracelet, a cat and a dog. She then wanted an envelope to put each picture in and wanted to write a letter on each envelope. This was totally led by the child, but supported by the adults who provided the envelopes and modelled the letter formation. It was a challenging task for Kayrah, but one in which she was deeply involved, operating at the limit of her capabilities and happy. For another child, the detail and control shown in the drawing below was equally challenging and the level of involvement equally high. Both are making progress in their 'literacy' development.

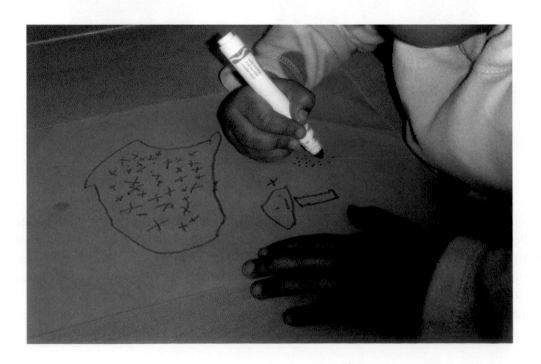

As the autumn term comes to an end, we are delighted with the progress that the children have made and confident that the provision is meeting their needs. We continue to focus on personal and social skills, recognising this as a prerequisite for all learning, but progress in all areas is evident. The children are very aware of text and the possibilities that reading and writing can offer. Nearly all activities develop language, most support the development of confidence and independence and many lead to improved physical skills – all of which will benefit the literacy skills in years to come. The children and staff are ready for a break – a chance to recharge, ready for the New Year.

5 January

The start of the spring term will see the need for reminders about expectations and boundaries. The children have had two weeks away from nursery, with lots of individual attention, possibly presents and a different routine. It usually takes about a week to re-establish the calm atmosphere that was created in the autumn term. This is a good time to remind staff about their role, and I explain this later in this chapter. I also describe our approach to class displays. In the environment section, I look at the opportunities for physical development, both indoors and outside. This includes a detailed explanation about woodwork and how, in fact, this can contribute to the development of all areas of learning. In the diary section, I have chosen some events to demonstrate the range of activities that occur every day in the nursery, illustrating that (even with no written forward planning) we don't have any problem covering the whole curriculum.

JANUARY: TO DO LIST

- Re-establish routines, boundaries and expectations after the holiday.
- Start second cycle of focus children.
- Start second cycle of parent meetings.
- Remind staff about their roles and deliver training if necessary

The role of the adult

The role of the adult in an early years setting is extremely complex and many books have been written on this subject alone. Throughout this book, there are descriptions of the numerous and varied roles of the adults in nursery. It is helpful to think about what we are trying to achieve (for the children to make outstanding progress) and then think about what we do as adults to support that. The list is long:

- Know, understand and support each unique child.
- Know, understand and work in partnership with each family.
- Organise an enabling environment that meets the needs and interests of each child.
- Understand child development to ensure appropriate challenge.
- Engage in quality interactions (teaching) to move learning forward.
- Ensure children are safe and cared for.
- Maintain records of assessment and progress.
- Reflect, review and amend provision and practice as appropriate.

Most of these roles involve work or study outside of the nursery session times. The most crucial role during session times is to engage in quality interactions with the children – it is this that makes the most difference to their learning and development. Again, whole books have been written on this subject. In Chapter 2: October, I described a few inter-actions and the learning that resulted. It is difficult to explain how to ensure quality is achieved so that learning results, but there are a few guidelines. The adult needs to:

1   be with the child;
2   like and be fascinated by the child;
3   give the child time to reveal their interests and ideas;
4   observe carefully and spot a 'teachable moment';
5   contribute to the activity in a way that is appropriate and in line with the wishes of the child;
6   match the body language, tone and voice level of the child;
7   use pondering questions.

An adult who is sat by their desk, 'barking' commands across the room is unlikely to contribute to any learning or development. In contrast, this photo shows Jacqui with Malachai – fascinated by him, willing to give him time, explaining how he can take a photo, allowing him to try various buttons, matching his body language, tone and voice level and extending his thinking about what to do with the photos he is taking. A skil-ful adult, therefore, ensures that every interaction results in progress and this is their most important role.

Many adults feel safe and confident if they are asked to lead a 'focus activity'. As explained earlier in the book, we have focus children, but **we do not have pre-planned focus activities**. This can be quite daunting for new adults. If you visited the nursery, you might well assume that all the adults had been given an activity to complete, but that is not the case. The staff will observe carefully and join groups in their chosen activity if they feel they can enhance the activity in any way. There are numerous examples of this throughout the book. I often visit settings where the lowest levels of involvement are seen at 'focus activities' – where the children have been called away from something that fascinates them to do something that is quite often mundane and not of great interest. In addition, if adults are occupied with a focus task, they will miss many 'teachable moments' in other parts of the nursery. They will also be unavailable to support children in their play, and if the children encounter a problem or if there is a dispute, the play might deteriorate. In contrast, at Carterhatch, the adults are free to enhance and support the play (overcoming problems to allow the play to develop further) and to help the children learn how to resolve disputes should they arise. Thus the play remains purposeful and calm with progress and learning happening constantly.

In many settings, the practitioners make notes, for example, 'Arda was looking at the guinea pig and asking his friend about the names of various parts on its body'. They would also note a 'next step': 'show the guinea pig to the children and point out his ears, nose', etc. When working 'in the moment', Jacqui was able to respond immediately when these boys showed an interest in the guinea pig, the vocabulary and information was shared and the teaching was powerful. No need for a next step – it had already been done.

Children are operating at the limit of their capabilities when they are deeply involved in an activity. Such deep-level involvement occurs when the children are allowed to initiate their own activity. The learning and development can be hindered whenever the child encounters an obstacle – perhaps they do not know how to use a tool, they don't know how to negotiate with other children, they can't reach something or they are not yet developmentally able to complete one part of the task. When these obstacles arise, the skilful adult will spot them and see them as teachable moments, moments in which they can join the child, provide the appropriate 'teaching' in order for the obstacle to be overcome, and then stand back and allow the child to continue. Thus the deep-level involvement is maintained and the learning is maximised. This is the most crucial role of an adult in any early years setting – it is indeed the most crucial role for any adult in education.

Class displays

I rarely think about displays but am often asked about them. For the most part, displays do not support the progress or development of the children in nursery. I visit many settings and often see displays that have clearly taken hours to prepare, but which the children barely notice. Visiting adults and parents do look at such displays, but not the children. There are a few exceptions. The display that is most valued by the nursery children is the world map, surrounded by pictures of children and their families as seen here.

The other displays that they look at regularly are the visual timetable and the self-registration board. We therefore keep other display boards simple and use them to show visitors the process of events that have taken place, often with photos of the children playing and deeply involved in activities. We also include speech bubbles with comments from the children and sometimes a few finished products as shown below.

Time is precious and I constantly assess what is valuable, in terms of its impact on the children. Hours spent on complex displays do not deliver dramatic impact on the learning in the nursery, and therefore we do not stress over this aspect of our work.

Setting up the environment

Physical development

Physical development happens in almost every area and every activity in the nursery – from the gross motor skills of climbing and running outside to the fine motor skills seen with sewing and drawing. Many of the resources are covered in the description of other areas of the nursery (water, creative, sand, digging, etc.) and therefore in this section I look at just a few areas that are primarily focused on physical development.

Outdoors – gross motor skills

I am generally opposed to fixed climbing structures (except monkey bars) because they are usually incredibly expensive, they may lack challenge and they take up a lot of space. At Carterhatch, we are very fortunate that space is not an issue and the fixed climbing apparatus is very challenging. It was, however very expensive, but was installed in the days when school budgets were far more generous. We have very few rules in the nursery, but one is that **when children are climbing, nobody touches anyone**. This includes adults – we do not touch the children as they climb. If they cannot climb up unaided, then they don't climb up! In this way, they can only climb as far as they are capable and are less likely to get stuck or to climb to a place that is not safe. I have often seen children fall when they are being 'held' by an adult, whereas if they are left alone, their concentration is far greater and they are less likely to fall. We do not have an adult stationed at the climbing structure but adults scan the whole area regularly and will intervene if necessary.

The photo below shows part of the nursery fence with hand and foot holds that have been attached to create a climbing wall. This is a cheap and simple way to add challenge if you have a fence like this.

Adults never touch the children when they are climbing, even if they ask for help to get up. In this way, they learn to concentrate and rely only on their own ability when climbing. They are then limited by their ability and less likely to climb too high and have an accident.

Other climbing apparatus includes A-frames, gym tables, ladders, logs, nesting tables and the large blocks.

The equipment is always available at the edge of this play area but it is up to the children if they want to set it up and in what configuration. When this is done, the staff are on hand to encourage the children to check the safety and to think about the space carefully. Sometimes the area will be used for other activities and again this is seen as a teachable moment when the children can learn to negotiate about the use of the space and come to some compromise.

The wheeled vehicles are another important resource in the development of gross motor skills, spatial awareness and balance. They are also available every day, but in a restricted area so that they do not disrupt other activities. As stated above, we are lucky with space, but in any setting, if the bikes are dominating the garden, then review the provision and consider their value in terms of learning. Again we use levels of involvement on wheeled toys. If the children are riding round with little challenge and low-level involvement, then perhaps the toys are not challenging enough. We have trikes, two-wheeled 'glider' bikes and two-wheeler pedal bikes. This range provides challenge for all the children.

As I write this page, I have just got home with another bike in my car – I saw it beside a bin outside a house. The owners were hoping someone would take it before the dustmen! I was happy to oblige. It is always worth keeping an eye out for abandoned treasures!

Small PE apparatus is also stored outside and available as part of the continuous provision. This includes balls of various sizes, stilts, skipping ropes, hoops, bats, ball catchers, bean bags, large skittles etc.

Woodwork

The other area outside that promotes physical development is the woodwork bench. However, this activity does in fact promote learning in all areas.

Whenever I deliver training, I am often asked about risk assessments. Risk assessments by their nature focus on the negative aspects of an activity. I always prefer to write a 'Benefit/Risk Assessment'. In this way, we focus on why we are doing a particular activity before thinking about the possible risks and how to mitigate them. The assessment below demonstrates that the benefits of woodwork clearly outweigh the risks.

Benefits

Woodwork is the perfect activity in which children can demonstrate the characteristics of effective learning:

- playing and exploring – children investigate and experience things, and 'have a go';
- active learning – children concentrate and keep on trying if they encounter difficulties, and enjoy achievements;
- creating and thinking critically – children have and develop their own ideas, make links between ideas, and develop strategies for doing things.

Also all the seven areas of learning in the current EYFS framework will be developed:

- *Physical development*: With the use of real tools and hard wood (rather than balsa wood), the muscles in the hands and arms become stronger and the children develop more control of these muscles. They learn to vary the amount of force used with hammers and saws. They also develop hand–eye coordination in order to hit the nails. Fine motor control is developed as children hold the thin

nails in place. Through experience they learn how to keep their fingers out of the way of the hammer.

- *Personal, social and emotional development*: Children demonstrate deep levels of involvement when undertaking a woodwork task. It is often noticeable that children who normally will not persevere at a task are prepared to try for far longer at woodwork – perhaps because they realise it is something truly challenging but also 'real'. Children will return to unfinished work the following day if necessary. They learn to share and take turns, negotiating and discussing routines and rules. They learn how to keep themselves and others safe. They realise that a real hammer can do serious harm and they treat the tools with respect. They learn to follow agreed rules. Children who find it difficult to conform are often so keen to participate that they manage to comply with requests and boundaries at the woodwork bench – just so that they get their turn. They take great pride in their achievements and therefore their self-esteem is boosted. For most children woodwork is a new activity and therefore they are taking a risk just by becoming involved. They take further risks using the equipment but learn to do this safely and independently and the results are greatly appreciated.
- *Communication and language development*: There is always a lot of discussion at the workbench and therefore language is developed. Children have to follow instructions and will often be heard explaining the rules to other children. They encounter problems all the time and discuss solutions. They explain what they are doing and learn the vocabulary associated with the activity.

- *Creative development*: With many activities for young children, the process is as important (if not more important) than the product. This is definitely the case when children are first starting at woodwork. They need to develop the techniques. Eventually, they will start to use their imagination, combined with their knowledge of the task, to plan what to make. With support, they will have learnt how it is possible to combine various materials and media and this will increase their options and possibilities. Many of the models become the starting point for a story that also supports creative development (as well as language skills).

- *Knowledge of the world*: Clearly through working with wood, the children will learn about its properties and the properties of other materials that they combine with the wood. They will learn about how to use tools and how to combine different materials. With appropriate interactions, they could learn about the source of wood and various types of wood. They will be experiencing the process of 'design, make, review'.
- *Mathematical development*: This pervades every aspect of the task – from experiencing the weight and size of the wood to deciding how many wheels to add to a truck. Children will be thinking about size and shape, as well as number. Again, with appropriate interaction, their thoughts can be vocalised, refined and developed.

- *Literacy development*: Children will often combine mark-making with woodwork – adding drawn features to their models. They also add their name to ensure their work is not lost. They will use books to refer to for ideas or information. Also, as mentioned above, many models will feature in stories and the literacy possibilities within this are infinite.

Figure 5.1 Benefits of woodwork

There are not many activities that appeal to so many children and have such broad and deep learning potential as woodwork.

Hazard	Possible scale of injury	Precautions to put in place to reduce risk	Risk rating
General risk of injury through use and misuse of tools	Medium	Staff will ensure that children are closely supervised during the induction period until all children have been trained in the use of the tools and comply with the 'two children at each bench' rule. Staff will then remain vigilant in watching the woodwork area. Adults all aware of how to get first aid help if necessary.	Low
Children with behavioural difficulties/ developmental delay might not adhere to the rules and might not use the tools safely	Medium	Staff will ensure close supervision of these children if they are near the woodwork area.	Low
Sawdust in eyes	Low	Children to wear goggles.	Low
Hit fingers with hammer	Low	Train children to tap lightly to fix nail in place and then move hand away when they hit harder.	Low
Children get hit by moving tools	Medium	Strict imposition of two children only limit at the bench. Staff will be scanning and monitoring the area at all times.	Low
Cut with saw	Low	Strict rule: 'wood in vice'.	Low
Splinters	Low	Wood will be checked. Children shown how to use sandpaper.	Low
Sharp nails cause injury	Low	Protruding nails will be hammered down. Children will not remove nails from work area.	Low

Figure 5.2 Risks of woodwork and appropriate actions

Clearly the benefits are great and the risks can be managed. (It should be noted that we have never had any serious accidents at the woodwork benches and rarely have even minor incidents.)

Practicalities

Here are some of the practicalities to consider:

- *Induction and access*: The bench is outdoors (the noise would be unbearable indoors) and in an area that can be seen at all times. When the children first start in the nursery, woodwork is available immediately and we have an adult beside the bench at all times. We encourage parents to help ensure that the children adhere to the very simple rules: two children at the bench, two hands on the saw. There is zero tolerance of any dangerous behaviour and the children quickly learn to behave appropriately if they want to be involved. The woodwork is part of our continuous, outstanding provision – it is always available and, therefore, does not cause a 'mad rush' to have a turn. After the induction period, adults keep an eye on the woodwork area, but an adult is not always stationed there.

- *Equipment*: I would recommend small claw hammers, smooth fine nails (bought by the kilo from an ironmonger) and adult-size hack saws (saws are not essential and many wonderful models can be made without a saw). The workbench from Creative Cascade UK Ltd is sturdy and a very reasonable price at £175. If the bench is not under a shelter, then cover with a tarpaulin at night or in heavy rain.

- *Additional resources*: We add a variety of resources for children to fix to the wood such as milk bottle tops, elastic bands, fabric, corex, corks, string etc. Paint, felt pens and pencils are available to decorate models as well. A good way to store these is in an Ikea rail attached to the end of the workbench.

● *Wood*: Wood is too expensive to buy. The best option is to find a local timber merchant who offers a 'cutting service' for customers. They are usually happy to keep off-cuts for use in school – we have taken a large bin to the timber yard that they fill up and we collect the wood every few weeks.

Woodwork leads to deep learning and outstanding progress in all areas of development. Children are attracted to the challenges it brings and fascinated by the possibilities. I often meet adults in other settings who are anxious about this activity but I would urge people to have a go – the resulting engagement and learning will amaze and delight adults and children alike.

Indoors – fine motor skills

Much of the development of fine motor skills occurs in the creative areas that are described in Chapter 6: February, and includes mark-making and sewing. As stated above, physical development occurs in almost all areas. For example, in the role play areas, the challenge of dressing a doll requires great dexterity and coordination – the concentration seen in this photo is a great example – Olivia's brain is lit up – progress is happening at this moment.

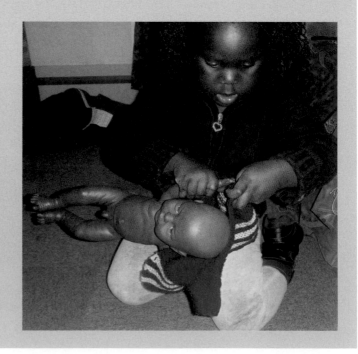

Playdough

As described in Chapter 3: November, there are continuous mathematical opportunities that arise with playdough. The physical development is also evident and valuable. Because it is so popular, we have one table that is just for playdough with the resources stored on a shelving unit just beside the table. This picture shows what is available and the unit is 'shadowed' to ensure resources are tidied easily when children have finished playing. The basket at the bottom contains a variety of cooking role play resources and various rolling pins. The contents of the basket can be supplemented if levels of involvement drop – for example we can add natural resources such as shells and stones and other items to promote numeracy, such as numicon pieces. The cooker hob can be removed from the shelf and used on the table.

Note the dust pan and brush hanging on the side of the unit – handy for sweeping up the crumbs that fall.

'Less is more' applies to this unit. We have just a few cutters – carefully chosen, rather than 30. The scissors can be used to cut playdough with ease – a good way to practise cutting and to experience success with this skill. A recipe for playdough is available in Appendix E.

This creation is 'Rapunzel'! It is a good example to show how young children do not segment their learning and how limiting it can be if we, as adults, try to impose a learning objective onto an activity. When Melisa made this she was developing PSE skills (having an idea, persevering, sharing resources); physical skills (rolling, cutting etc.); language skills (talking about her model); literacy skills (retelling the story of Rapunzel and later dictating a story to an adult); maths skills (symmetry, length, shape etc.); understanding the world (using tools, understanding different materials etc.) and creative skills (using her imagination and representing her ideas).

Diary extracts: Examples of development and learning

WHAT TO LOOK OUT FOR

- Children settle back into nursery routines quickly after the holiday.
- Children begin to follow 'themes' in their play.
- More children play in groups, rather than alongside each other.
- Children learn from each other.
- Parents are delighted with the progress that their children are making.

Curriculum coverage

As described above, whenever a child accesses the woodwork then they are immediately covering a wide range of areas of development. Various modes of transport are often a theme in the play of nursery children – some of which are within their experience, such as cars and buses. Abdulkadir chose to make a train and in the process he improved his physical skills, he experienced mathematical concepts, he was creative in the design, he persevered, he was proud of the final product and he was able to talk about his model.

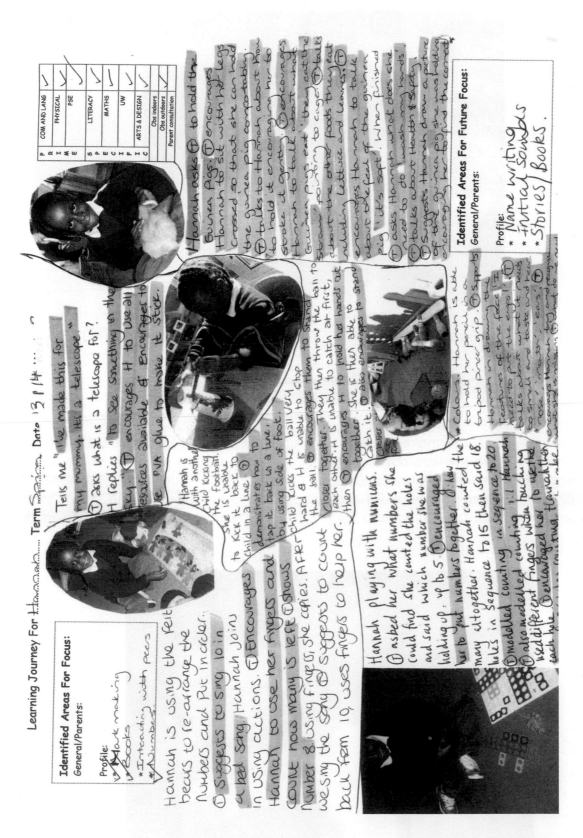

Figure 5.3 Sample learning journey for January

Note: See Chapter 2: October for explanation.

The transport theme continued when Rayan made a helicopter pad with the blocks.

Later Guiseppe wanted to make a paper aeroplane that he had seen some older children playing with. He had the idea but without adult support at that moment, he would not have been able to complete his plan. Once he had been shown how to fold the paper, he was able to help other children make their planes. He added windows and, again at the suggestion of an adult, he dictated a short story that was acted out at the end of the session.

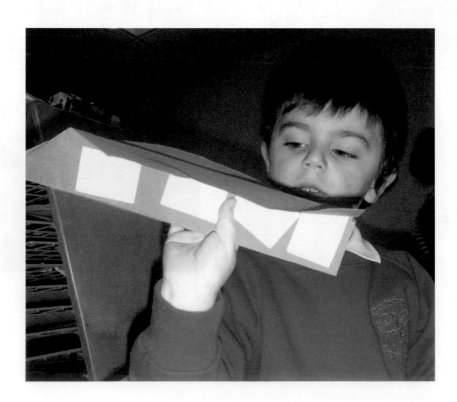

The wet weather in early 2014 caused floods in many parts of the country. In London, the rain was persistent and the puddles presented further learning opportunities. In some settings the rain means that the doors are closed and everyone stays indoors. However, with the right attitude from the staff, the learning can continue. The puddles were used as lakes and the fishing nets were much more challenging and fun to use.

There were further discussions about the flooding and how some people were having to go to school by boat. I had been given a boat by my neighbour, which is located in the reception garden and so an adult suggested taking a group to play in this real boat. This gave the children first-hand experiences of being in the reception garden (where most of them will be in September) and the feel of a real boat (even though it was not on water!).

Once in the boat, there were inevitable games involving sharks and fish and how to catch them. One of the boys started to talk about the fish he had at home and once back in nursery, Eren started to draw some fish. Rachel suggested they make a fishing game and so several fish were drawn, paper clips added and then the fishing rods were made.

In this sequence, as is often the case with young children, the play covered numerous areas of development. PSE and language development pervade all activities as children initiate ideas, take risks, feel good and talk about what they are doing. In this case the physical development is clear – pencil control, cutting and then coordinating the rods to catch the fish. There was creative development in the design of the fish and learning related to magnets when the paper clips were added. Maths was involved in discussions about the length of string, how many fish were caught and the size and shape of the fish. There were many boating and fishing stories created in the next few weeks as well as books, such as Mr Gumpy's Outing being chosen. The literacy links are therefore evident as well.

Several children have come into nursery with new hairstyles and this has sparked an interest in hairdressers. Therefore the 'pop up' role play area has become a hairdressers. Role play again covers numerous areas of development. The levels of involvement will be monitored and the area will be changed when the children lose interest.

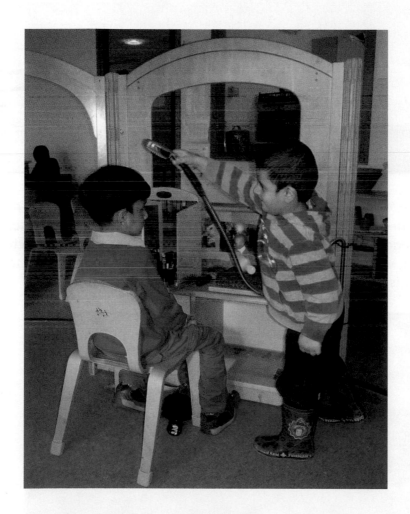

Many children are interested in dinosaurs in the nursery and there are plenty for them to play with. The children are also interested in the numicon and it has been fascinating to see these two resources being used together. One child noticed that the numicon piece for 3 looked like a 'leg'. With encouragement from Jacqui, the children started to see what the other numicon pieces could be and to build a dinosaur with them. The discussions revolved around the size of the parts of the body and the size of the numicon pieces. The link became clear that the bigger body parts needed a bigger piece of numicon – i.e. a higher number. The resulting models were wonderful!

As stated in the 'What to look out for' list – the children are definitely playing in groups and pairs far more now, rather than alongside each other. The conversations that are overheard are often delightful. The three pictures below show children interacting and learning from each other, without any adult nearby. Once this starts to happen, the learning potential in the class is huge and certainly something to celebrate.

'This is how you put your shoe on. You need to open the straps first. Now push your foot in!'

'You need to just walk on your toes. Try to step on every log.'

'Show me your family. Do you have a sister?'

What is very noticeable at the end of January is how the classes have 'jelled' and how different sessions vary according to the groups that are attending. There are strong friendships forming – pairs and groups – and the children are benefitting from the help, support and conversation they get from their peers as well as from the adults. The curriculum is being covered with ease – a clear indication that the provision is appropriate. Everyone is hoping for some dry, warm weather – but the children continue to explore and learn, whatever the weather!

6 | February

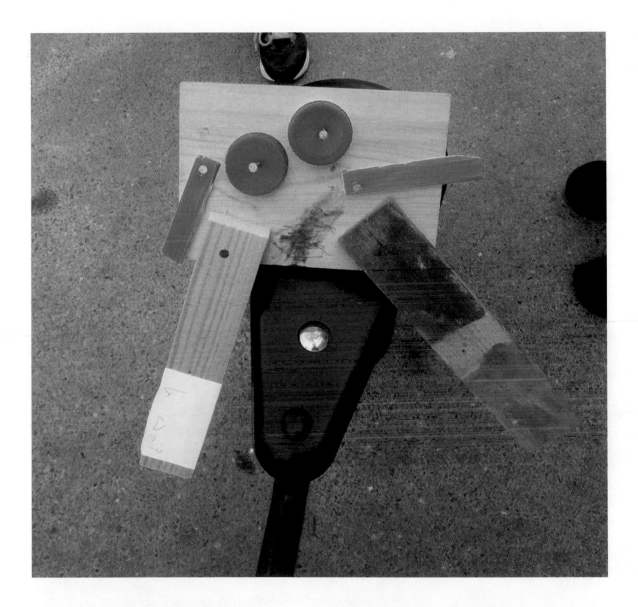

Over the next few months, there is a period when we can totally focus on the learning and development of the current cohort of children because they are completely settled, we know them so well and we are not yet planning for next year. It is during these months that we see the children progress in sudden leaps. Children that have been quietly absorbing all that is going on will suddenly demonstrate their abilities. For practitioners, it is often tempting to try and force children to display their abilities, but it is always preferable to wait for them to do this voluntarily. In this chapter, I describe our ever-changing approach to information and communication technologies (ICT) and how we deal with toilet training. In the environment section I explain the organisation of the creative areas both indoors and outside and also the snack area. The diary gives some examples of the more unusual first-hand experiences that happened this month and a few of the 'Wow!' moments that highlight some of the leaps that the children are making.

FEBRUARY: TO DO LIST

- Continue with second cycle of focus children.
- Continue with second cycle of parent meetings.
- Celebrate the numerous 'Wow!' moments that occur.
- Remember to offer the children as many new first-hand experiences as possible.
- Don't forget – children have a natural desire to explore and learn – trust them!

ICT

ICT covers a broad range of activities and equipment. I look first at the aspect of technology that is causing practitioners the most concern – screens – on PCs, tablets, phones, game consoles etc. As I have stated, we use levels of involvement to assess whether an activity is engaging and valuable for the children. A child can appear to be deeply involved when operating a game on a screen.

However, recent brain scan research has shown that, in fact, when using screen technology, only a small part of the brain is 'lit up', rather than the large areas that are lit up during other activities, such as building a den or using a hammer and nails. The addictive nature of such devices has also been proven, which will come as no surprise to many who have watched children become more and more obsessed with screen-based activities. We must then question and re-evaluate their use in our settings.

When evaluating screen use in school, we should also take into account the amount of time that children are spending looking at screens when not at school. When computers were first introduced to schools, it was something that many children would not have access to elsewhere. However, every mobile phone is now a powerful computer and 18 month old babies know how to access certain apps by touching screens. With so much exposure to ICT out of school, this again must make us re-evaluate its use in our settings.

One other factor is that, because of the increase in technology in the home, children are spending less time playing outdoors and playing with creative equipment (construction toys, art equipment etc.). Therefore it is even more important that educational settings offer the experiences that children are not getting at home. We need to increase the amount of active, creative, independent play that is not available elsewhere. Another reason to re-evaluate the use of screens.

The early learning goal for **technology** states: 'Children recognise that a range of technology is used in places such as homes and schools. They select and use technology for particular purposes'. This wider consideration of technology fits more comfortably in our approach.

We have two iPads that are used occasionally to play games (primarily related to literacy or maths) but more often they are used to take photos and videos and to look up information on the internet (rather like an instant encyclopaedia). We have an Interactive white board that is used to show photos from home, photos taken at school, video clips of nursery activities or from the Internet. It is also used with selected programmes – for example to develop drawing, number or phonic skills.

This group were attracted to the interactive white board (IWB) by the music – one child had started talking about their mum going to a Zumba class and so Jacqui found a video class that the children could join in with. The levels of involvement were high as the children were not sitting and just moving their fingers; they had to be up and active to copy the movements on the screen.

The digital cameras are in constant use in school and as mentioned in Chapter 2: October, a few children take a camera home each week. They are then involved in the processes of showing the pictures on a screen and selecting some to print. Once printed, they cut them out to stick in their 'special book'. The children often take pictures to print as part of a book or story as well. This 'instant' result is something that they accept as routine, unaware of just how recent this technology is.

We have other equipment in numerous areas of the nursery. Indoors there are digital clocks, programmable toys, CD players, door release buttons and a variety of role play equipment that requires technology – microwave, TV, kettle, toaster, cash register, remote control, mobile phone, iron, calculators, digital scales etc. Outdoors the cameras are still used, there is another CD player, metal detectors, walkie-talkies, telephones and further role play equipment.

Even without realistic props, the children will still demonstrate their understanding of the use of technology!

The one piece of equipment that we have decided to remove from the classrooms are the PCs. As a team, we felt that the problems caused by the PCs (in terms of supervision, arguments, obsessive behaviours) were not outweighed by the benefits. The iPads and the IWB can be used in the same way, but are far easier to remove or switch off, and iPads in particular are more versatile in their use.

These children are using the iPad to dictate a story to go along with the photos they have taken. This can then be shared with the whole class on the interactive white board during a carpet session. This is a good example of the versatility of this technology.

Toilet training

During my 25 years in teaching, I have seen an ever-increasing number of children who start nursery (and reception) without being toilet trained. Up until about six years ago, we were able to insist on children being out of nappies before they could start nursery. This was a massive incentive for parents to get on with the task of toilet training their children. However, now that we have to accept all children into nursery, the task is falling more and more to the staff in school. We try to work with the parents to develop a consistent approach: remove nappies during nursery sessions; take the child to the toilet every half hour or hour; praise them if they use the toilet; and deal with accidents with as little emotion and attention as possible. Jacqui and the staff tackle the training with one or two children at any one time. If they try to deal with more children than this, it becomes too time consuming. They have been very successful and all but one of the children are now able to manage their own toileting needs and are out of nappies.

Setting up the environment

Creative areas indoors and outside

Creative development covers numerous activities from role play, to painting, to singing, to making up stories. In this chapter I am concentrating on the 'art' aspect of creativity: mark-making, sewing, model-making etc.

Sewing equipment is available in the nursery. Young children constantly surprise me in the way they challenge themselves – in this case to make a bag! The adults are used by the children for the parts of the process that they cannot do independently – in this instance that included threading the needle and tying a knot in the thread but very little else.

As mentioned in Chapter 4: December, we don't have a 'writing area' because young children do not separate their learning and play into distinct subjects. They will make a beautiful card and then write a message inside; they will 'write' a shopping list and draw some of the items; they will make a robot, paint it and then 'write' a story about it. Mark-making will combine elements of drawing and writing and therefore all the resources are stored in one large area, with one large table. This is replicated outside, although with fewer collage materials as they blow away!

Restocking the creative areas is a time-consuming task. As with all areas the equipment is shadowed or labelled with a photo and word to ensure that the children can tidy up independently. Tilted storage boxes are useful for collage materials and the Ikea rails and pots are great for pencils and pens etc. but also for sewing equipment. Junk modelling boxes are displayed on shelves along with an assortment of paper and card. Other resources include scissors, sticky tape in dispensers, staplers, hole punches, sewing equipment, string, glue (various types), fabric and wool. There are also easels indoors and outside along with drying racks. At present, we are using ready mixed paint, but I am still hoping to find a system that allows the children to successfully mix their own powder paints. I did see nursery children dispensing powder paint stored in sugar shakers in Larkhill Nursery in Stockport – that's next on my wish list! Outside there is also a huge black board with chalks nearby and white boards with pens. There are clipboards that the children can move around the nursery so that they can in fact mark make anywhere.

Setting up the environment

Snack area

Since we want the children to be as independent as possible and to have long periods of time to get absorbed in their pursuits, we do not want to dictate when they have a drink or snack. Therefore we have a 'snack area' where a few children can go at any time to have a drink (of water or milk) and a snack of fruit or salad items (carrots or tomatoes).

Many settings still have whole class snack time and I have seen extremely low levels of involvement during such sessions as children wait for the bowl of fruit to reach them. Many practitioners worry that some children won't eat and that others will take too much. Surely this then is a teaching and learning opportunity. As I write this chapter, the snack area is totally self-regulating with children taking drinks and snacks that they need, without overeating.

Diary extracts: Examples of development and learning

WHAT TO LOOK OUT FOR

- All but a very few children are toilet trained.
- The children are very confident and independent – enjoying new experiences.
- Children settle back immediately after the half term break.
- Children apply their learning independently creating many 'Wow!' moments.

As usual, with such a busy nursery, it is very difficult to select events to include in the diary. In this chapter I have included some of the more unusual first-hand experiences that are so important because of the way they engage the children and give them activities, memories and experiences that will enrich their play and imagination. In addition, I have included some of the 'Wow!' moments that are happening throughout the nursery at this time of the year.

First-hand experiences

Everything that happens in nursery is a first-hand experience: they are not just *told* how to make a cake, they do it; they do not just *watch* the adults dig, they join in; they don't just *look* at the climbing equipment, they climb on it; they don't just *read* about snails, they find them and touch them. This is how young children learn. They are not able to take in information and ideas in an abstract format – they have to **experience them**. For example, we can tell children the best way to make a sand castle, but it is only by having a go that they will learn how to make a sand castle. Theory of mind shows that children become able to take in ideas in a more abstract form after the age of about five or six. This, then, is why it is so important that the early years remain play-based with first-hand experiences being paramount.

In addition to the continuous provision, there are always opportunities to extend the experiences as interests arise or events occur. For example, the children were pretending to be at a café when playing with the playdough. A trip to the local café meant that the play and conversations were far more realistic the next day.

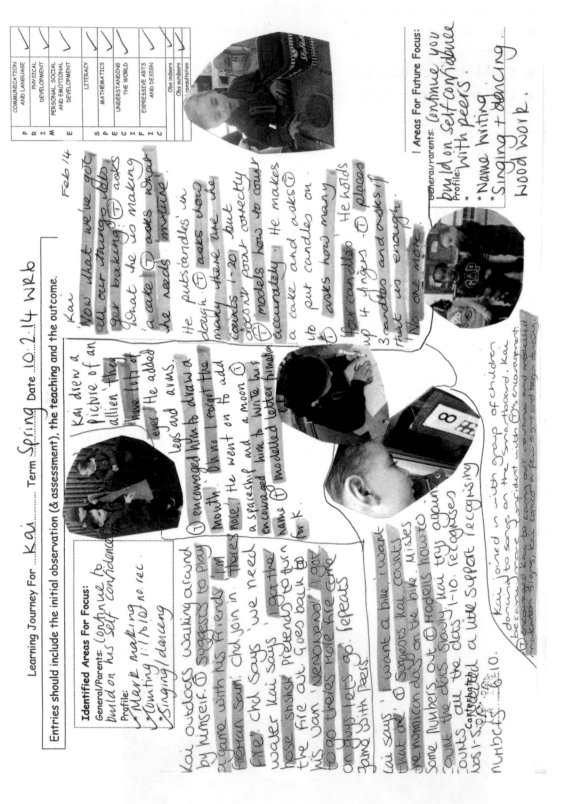

Figure 6.1 Sample learning journey for February

Note: See Chapter 2: October for explanation.

In the moment Planning - Nursery

W/C: 2|12|13 Term: Week: 14 Page: 2

Carterhatch

Focus Children:

* * * *

* * * *

	PRIME AREAS			SPECIFIC AREAS			
	C&L	PHD	PSE	LIT	MATHS	UW	EXP A&D
	✓	✓	✓	✓	✓	✓	✓

Monday	Tuesday	Wednesday	Thursday	Friday

	Observation and Assessment	(Plan and) Teaching	Outcome (Observation)
1:	Chd wanted to make a car.	T encouraged them to use all the blocks, tyres and bumper. Children role played going to the cinema and the chicken shop	
2:	Children are reading books and ask T to sit so they can be read to her.	T Encouraged children to describe what they could see in the pictures to help them tell the story	
3:	Chd on climbing frame talking about going to the moon.	T Encourages chd to sing 'zoom zoom we going to the moon' encourages children to use their fingers to count. Encourages EAL chd to use their words while singing and counting. Count down from 5, then count to 10, then count back down from 10.	Sing at carpet time
4:	chn wanted to be teachers.	T gave them her Makaton symbols & encouraged them to take turns at being Jaqui counting - language signing	Make set of symbols & leave for children to us
5:	chd building bridge to walk.	T Encourages chd to think about how to make it safe to walk along thinking about how many logs to put on top of each other and how to make them balance.	
6:	Chn playing at exercise classes.	T Encourages them to take turns leading the class & feel their hearts after each exercise to see how fast it beat	

Photo's

Figure 6.2 Sample 'Planning in the moment' sheet

Similarly, the fascination with cars is always enhanced by the chance to sit in a real car and look at the engine.

The model cars that were built in the days following this little expedition were far more sophisticated.

Many of the children in nursery enjoy role playing family situations with babies and caring for babies generally. While many of the children do have younger siblings, others do not. Any time that a baby can be 'borrowed' from one of the parents is a great opportunity for all the children to examine these tiny people and learn a little more about their needs and abilities.

As mentioned above, all the experiences in nursery are 'first-hand' or 'hands-on'. The cameras are no exception. By purchasing tough cameras, we can let the children use them independently and experience the results of their efforts.

The cameras that we have purchased are Olympus Tough. They are taken home by the focus children at the weekends but also used in school by staff and children during the week.

'Wow!' moments

To finish this chapter, I present just a few of the many 'Wow!' moments (see Chapter 3: November) that were noted in nursery this month. In each case, I have included the photo and the short comment added by the practitioner that clarifies why it was a special moment or might give some context to the photo.

Aiden persevered for over 20 minutes to complete this line of bottle tops. He then started to count them and counted with 1–1 correspondence to 19. (Both the period of concentration and the accurate counting were things of note for this child.)

The shadowing for the blocks can be seen clearly on this shelving unit.

Edona built this zoo over a period of about 40 minutes. She knew all the names of the animals and also knew which animals needed to be kept away from others 'in case they eat them!'. (Edona has often played with the animals and adults have been commentating and joining her in these games. Today she independently repeated much of the information they have been giving her.)

The storage unit seen in this picture is from Ikea – very cheap but sturdy and perfect for storing a selection of resources to be used on the carpet. The top can be used to keep or display work and is also strong enough to sit on.

Rio and Nadir played together to build the train track right across the carpet. They then took a few trains each and played with them on the track that they had built. (Both these boys have found it quite challenging to share the space and resources in nursery. This event was noteworthy because it showed progress in their personal and social skills.)

Olivia displayed an understanding of writing when she produced this 'story'. She 'wrote' from left to right, and top to bottom, saying the words as she wrote. She left some gaps in the writing and included a few recognisable letters. (This was the first occasion that Olivia had been seen to do this. She had watched adults scribe stories [see Chapter 4: December] and this was the evidence to show that she saw herself as a writer and also that she was indeed developing many of the skills of a writer.)

Gullu demonstrated leadership skills when she acted as 'teacher' to this group – teaching them the English words for numerous items in this book. As each new word was introduced, she insisted that each boy repeat it in English! (Gullu has clearly been absorbing lots of English but this was the first occasion when she had been seen teaching other children.)

Kiara has been a little worried about a hospital visit that is going to happen in the near future. She worked with a group of children to make this 'hospital' and because she was the 'expert', she was able to explain all the different areas that were needed. Through this activity she was able to talk about what would happen at the hospital and seemed reassured by this. (Although reluctant to talk about the hospital, Kiara demonstrated a great deal of knowledge about different aspects of hospital activity during this game.)

Rayhan was able to use the camera independently today. He also wrote all the letters for his name on the finished story. (Rayhan has produced other stories and therefore the story scribing is not necessarily a 'Wow!' moment. However, this was the first time he had used the camera confidently and independently. It was also the first time that he had managed to include all the letters for his name.)

Muhammet was seen mark-making today – drawing a dinosaur. He was concentrating for about 10 minutes at this task. (Muhammet has rarely opted to mark-make and therefore this event was noteworthy for him. The choice and concentration are the 'Wow!' events, rather than the product.)

Kayra decided independently to make signs for the vegetables that she had helped to plant in the garden. Her phonic skills have improved in recent weeks, allowing her to attempt complex words. This photo is also evidence of her drawing skills. (This photo must be accompanied by annotation so that it is clear that Kayra produced this writing independently – using and applying her phonic skills. It should also be noted that only a few children in nursery would be at this level.)

Maria managed to produce an extended story today by using images from magazines as a stimulus for new ideas. (Maria has been writing several stories, but many have been very short and all similar to each other. This story broke the pattern and was noteworthy for that reason.)

A simple and cheap way to make a stage is to get two pallets and then screw lengths of decking onto them and along the front and sides.

Kaan was observed singing along in English on the stage – joining in with songs that the class have been learning recently. (Kaan has been listening to the songs at group time, but has not joined in when it was a large group. This event was then noteworthy because he felt confident to sing the songs in this smaller group outside.)

It is very important to keep paperwork to a manageable level. One way to help with this is to ensure that what we write is meaningful and useful. I often visit settings where all the adults are constantly making observations and this concerns me greatly for two main reasons: first these observations are often mundane and repetitive (not serving any purpose – either in terms of ideas for future learning or as evidence of any 'Wow!' moments) and second (and most importantly), while adults are writing observations, they are **not interacting with the children**. It is estimated that an early years practitioner has over 1,000 interactions per day. If they were to write down each interaction, this number reduces to below 100. So we can have 1,000 interactions – (ie 1,000 episodes of teaching and impact on progress); or less than 100. So let's write less and interact more!

As February comes to an end, we are over half way through the year and Jacqui and the team have 60 children to observe and assess – meaning paperwork is a huge task. On checking the files, I am confident that we are gathering enough evidence about these amazing children. During sessions the adults are interacting with the children and observing as well. They are writing the truly noteworthy events – keeping the paperwork meaningful and (almost) manageable.

7 March

As with February, the children continue to take leaps in their learning throughout March. What is most striking is the level of complexity that appears in their play, the length of time that activities last and also the number of children involved. A few such events are described in the diary section. To start the chapter, I briefly touch on risk assessments (or rather benefit assessments). Since the end of the spring term is usually near the end of March, I summarise the data again to indicate the general progress of this cohort. In the environment section I describe the ways in which we support investigation of the natural world, our music provision and cooking.

MARCH: TO DO LIST
● Continue second cycle of focus children.
● Continue second cycle of parent meetings.
● Update, summarise and evaluate assessments for the Easter break.

Benefit/risk assessments

This rope and the trapeze rings are in the reception garden and the nursery children get a chance to play on them during transition visits to their new classes.

As mentioned in Chapter 5: January, we no longer write risk assessments at Carterhatch, rather we write 'benefit/risk assessments' for activities and equipment (such as for the rope swing above). This means that we consider and list the benefits of the equipment or activity and then any risks that might be incurred. If we can't think of enough benefits, then we would consider removing the equipment or not undertaking a particular activity. Trikes in a reception class are a good example of equipment that is not very beneficial (reception children display low levels of involvement when riding trikes) – whereas they do still challenge and engage nursery age children. It can be interesting to write such documents as a team as it makes practitioners re-evaluate accepted practices in a new way. It is also valuable to do this when considering trips out of nursery or new activities in nursery. If parents (or sometimes management) are anxious about an activity, but you can demonstrate the learning and development that it will bring, then they are more likely to feel positive about it.

Data update

With the end of the spring term approaching, we update the data on progress using our usual format (see Figure 7.1).

Nursery	% well below expected level	% below expected level	% at expected level	% above expected level
Entry September 2013	37	43	15	5
Term 1 December 2013	22	42	31	5
Term 2 March 2014	18	34	41	7

Figure 7.1 Term 2 progress data for OFSTED

Setting up the environment

Investigation

Children are investigating from the moment they arrive in nursery – whether it be the effect of paint, the noise of a drum or how it feels to jump off a log – but in this section, I am specifically going to look at the provision for investigating the natural world that can be found within the nursery environment.

Some children found this caterpillar and placed it on the 2D image of himself, or is it herself? I'm not sure – how can we find out? This is the sort of investigation that we want to promote – but in order for questions to be asked, the environment has to invite such curiosity. Even if there is no grass, soil or shrubs in a setting, it is possible to create areas that will attract minibeasts and it is possible to grow plants in raised beds or pots. Jacqui has created a wonderful 'bug hotel' using some logs, woodchip, straw and pieces of bamboo. It is possible to request logs and woodchip from your local parks department or a local tree surgeon. Once set up, depending on the weather and the state of the logs (the older, the better), bugs should appear within a few weeks.

Two of the boys in this picture have magnifying glasses. They were able to collect these easily from the investigation unit that is placed nearby.

On this unit there are magnets, binoculars, compasses, magnifying glasses, bug boxes, stopwatches, tape measures, walkie-talkies (no longer working, but the children don't seem to mind!) and tweezers. The basket of books contains reference books for various minibeasts and plants that the children might find. The books have to be put inside at night but the unit is left in place with the tarpaulin pulled over to keep the items dry. Again,

shadowing has been used to support the children in returning the objects to the shelf correctly. This is one of the units that we are hoping to replace – the shelves are too deep so that objects cannot easily be seen, and also it is not possible to add photos and captions at the back of the shelves. We always have a wish list and this is one item that is on there to be replaced.

The digging area with logs and stones also attracts worms and other creatures.

The water carrier (visible at the top of this photo) is a fantastic compromise if you don't have an outside tap or a water butt. It allows the children to access water independently.

We also have two guinea pigs in the nursery and our benefit/risk assessment comes down clearly in favour of having these animals in the class. The children learn first hand how to care for these pets and for many children it is the first chance they have had to hold a live animal. The RSPCA say that although they do not really like settings to have pets, they do say that guinea pigs are the most tolerant. Our guinea pigs seem very relaxed with the children as shown by their willingness to eat, even when on a child's lap.

Of course the main stimulus for investigation is a child's natural desire to explore and learn. They will be curious about things in the sky, on the ground, under the table, in their pocket – we cannot possibly predict what the next question might be. The adults then become key in supporting the children to find answers, either by encouraging them to explore further or by helping them look up answers in books or on the Internet. The growing area is of course a huge source of investigation and learning and is dealt with in detail in Chapter 9: May.

Setting up the environment

Music

Whole books have been written about the value of music and singing – and indeed the levels of involvement that we see during such sessions are always high. As mentioned in Chapter 4: December, we often use time during group sessions to sing songs. I play the guitar and whenever I am able to join the session, it increases the levels of involvement and enjoyment. You only need to play three chords to convince nursery children that you are a star musician, so I would urge practitioners to give it a go! We also have CD players, iPads and the interactive white board, which can all bring music into the classroom. In terms of musical instruments, as with all resources, the best option is to have these as part of the continual provision – i.e. they are available all the time. Because of the noise, the instruments are kept outdoors, next to the stage area (see photo on page 141 of Chapter 6: February) and again we use open shelving with laminated photos to store the resources.

The unit, as with several others, has a tarpaulin attached that is pulled over it at night. Instruments are very expensive (the bells seen here cost about £40) and we impress on the children that these resources cannot be transported around the setting and must be treated gently. In some settings, I have seen these bells jumbled up in a box with numerous other instruments. If they are displayed with care, then the children are more likely to treat them with care. In reception, we have added simple music scores above the shelf unit and children can then actually play the tune of *Twinkle Twinkle Little Star* or other simple songs.

Setting up the environment

Cooking

If you monitor how children play during their time in nursery, much of the role play will revolve around cooking – in the sand, water, mud, woodchip, home corner or the playdough area. It is something that all the children have in common – they all see someone cooking at home. Moving the play into real cooking brings numerous benefits and learning in all areas of development. We have one unit in the nursery class that is covered with a cloth and the children know that they cannot access this unit without permission. I have yet to find a way to have cooking available in our continuous provision but it is an activity that happens very often. We have aprons specifically for cooking and a regular delivery from a local supermarket keeps us stocked up with the basics. A trip to the local shop is a regular event to top up or buy special ingredients. A favourite activity is cake making using the tried and tested recipe of balancing eggs with flour, then with sugar and finally with margarine and then mixing the whole lot together (see Appendix F). If you watch the video available at www.freedomtolearn.co.uk/ links you will see some of the class making the cakes independently. Note also how all areas of development are covered in this one activity.

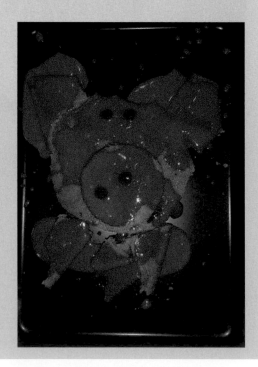

Diary extracts: Examples of development and learning

WHAT TO LOOK OUT FOR

- Children start to play in large groups.
- Games or scenarios become more complex.
- Time spent at any one activity is extended.

Complex, sustained, group play

This cohort of children have definitely started to form friendship groups and they are beginning to work cooperatively in their games. There were several examples of this seen in March and I describe just a few.

This morning a group of children found something fascinating in the garden. Questions and suggestions led the children to conclude that it was a mouse, and that it was definitely dead. The discussion then moved on to what to do about this. Rayhan knew that it had to be buried in a hole and Eren suggested that a good place would be under the bushes. The children fetched spades from the digging area and dug a hole. Jacqui pointed out that they should not touch any dead creatures as they might have serious germs that could make the children ill. Another discussion then took place as to how to move the mouse and the children decided to use a spade and to then wash the spade. The mouse was successfully buried and then Jacqui asked how they could stop other children digging in that spot.

Learning Journey For Rayhan .... Term Spring Date 3.3.14 WK 9

Entries should include the initial observation (& assessment), the teaching and the outcome.

	COMMUNICATION AND LANGUAGE	✓
P		
R	PHYSICAL DEVELOPMENT	✓
I		
M	PERSONAL, SOCIAL AND EMOTIONAL DEVELOPMENT	✓
S	LITERACY	✓
P	MATHEMATICS	✓
E		
C	UNDERSTANDING THE WORLD	✓
I		
F	EXPRESSIVE ARTS AND DESIGN	✓
I	Obs indoors	✓
C	Obs outdoors	✓
	Parent consultation	

Next Steps:
* Number recognition
* Name writing

Identified Areas For Focus:

General/Parents:

Profile:
* writing/markmaking
* Numbers
* Reading

Rayhan ... March ...
Plays ball with another child – shows excellent control of ball when kicking ball. Suggest he tries other ways to pass the ball. He is not so confident when throwing or catching ball. Makes good attempt to bounce. 'I play football with my dad.' He was happy to take turns and waited patiently for his turn.

Rayhan saw ① taking pictures, 'I want to picture.' ① gives Rayhan a please camera to take pictures ① shows Rayhan how to use the camera 'I press this button' (pointed at correct button) ① What pictures will you take? ② Rayhan went around the room and took pictures of various toys. 'I took it the picture' ① suggested to pick out the pictures and tell a story about his favourite toys. Rayhan agreed to this. After telling his story ① suggested to use his name tag to write his name. (can't do) ② focus's letter formation. forms lots of name and form letters in name.
and R. ① came to encourage Rayhan to write his name in name.

Rayhan was encouraged to tidy up with his friends. ① encouraged them to collect blocks and make pills to see who could make the... the tallest. Rayhan's was the smallest. 'Oh mine is not big' ① modelled language 'smallest and tallest' ① noticed the word 'tall.' in R.' ① encouraged him to count how many blocks he had collected counted 1,1,2,3,4,5.

'What's that mean?' 'It means you go to hospital. My dad told me you floor if it's in a wet floor... triangle it means you have and hurt your leg. to follow the instruction. Yeah, you need to be careful or...

Figure 7.2 Sample learning journey for March

Note: See Chapter 2: October for explanation.

Owen decided to make this X to indicate that no one should play or dig here. Discussions renewed the next day when the X had been ignored and the mouse was gone!

Today a group of children were enjoying their game as mechanics, fixing the never-ending queue of vehicles. An old bike stand had been dumped behind the school and the adults suggested this could be used to hold all the tools. This was so successful that the children wanted to keep it as part of the garden. Much discussion was had about where it could be placed. The children wanted it in the centre of the bike area – currently occupied by a small hill. However, Malachai pointed out that 'We can dig that and move it!'. So that is what they did, using adults for muscle and moving a large section of the hill, then putting the bike rack in its place along with a bench for customers to sit on (or as a bus stop).

The next series of photos shows a game that lasted a whole day and involved about 20 different children coming and going with various ideas and skills. I was reminded of a group of ants – all working away at the same task without any obvious discussion or plan beforehand. The children seemed to be aware of the plan and were deeply involved in their part. As with all activities, although this was not a planned focus activity, the adults were nearby, observing and supporting as necessary. For example, when a cooker was needed an adult had to agree that the unit could be moved from another part of the garden. However, for the most part, this amazing construction was completed independently by the children, with adults commentating and enjoying a very special event.

A few children start to enclose the blue mats to make a swimming pool, but then decide they are making a house.

Osuani decides to add 'flowers' around the edge. Notice the spanner and spirit-level being used for this large building project.

Thomas consults the plans to decide where the toilet should go!

The cable drum makes a good toilet – and it is so popular that there is a queue.

Alfie points out the exit route. Notice the stairs that have been built to enter the house.

Other children join the play and some decide to add extra features to the flowers.

Several boys work together to create a car – parked just next to the house.

Kiara decides the kitchen will not fit in the rooms they have made.

Finally, the kitchen extension has a wall to enclose it.

As March comes to an end, it is clear that the children are making rapid progress. What is striking from the examples in this diary section (and numerous others that I could have included) is that if we, the practitioners, had planned activities that the children had to do, then they would have missed out on so much. We would never plan to put a dead mouse in nursery, or dig up a hill or spend the whole day with 20 children constructing a complex role play area. And yet, we have seen this month that if we let the children decide what to do, they set themselves greater challenges, with huge ambition and amazing perseverance.

8 April

The Easter break usually takes up two weeks of April and therefore it is a short school month for the children. It is also the month when schools get their new budget and decisions can be made about spending. I explain briefly how we decide what to bid for from this new pot of money. In the environment section, I talk about our 'mud kitchen' and also the large construction area – both outside. The diary section gives further examples of sustained activity, this time I have also picked out examples where individuals have sustained their involvement at an activity, as well as group involvement.

APRIL: TO DO LIST
- Start third and final cycle of focus children.
- Start third and final cycle of parent meetings.
- Decide on priorities for any bids in the new budget.

Budget decisions

If you are lucky enough to have any money at all to spend, then take great care making decisions. Use levels of involvement to determine which sort of activities and resources engage the children the most – this indicates where the most powerful learning is happening and therefore where money should be spent. Also, buy open-ended resources, resources that can be used in hundreds, if not thousands of different ways – blocks, sand, water, creative resources, etc. If you have enough money to buy storage units, then look for inspiration in this book or in other settings – find out what works well. Once you analyse progress data or patterns, you might find that you need resources for one particular area. We have an ongoing wish list that we add to throughout the year. I would like some more of the concrete covered up in the garden – perhaps with high-quality fake grass, but that would cost thousands and is out of the question just now. However, it might be possible to use sleepers or logs as a boundary and fill an area with woodchip or bark to change the surface.

This is something that we did in the reception garden last year and the two photos below show how the area was transformed for very little cost.

Another item on the wish list is a rope swing and/or some monkey bars. This year, we have watched the children find numerous places where they can hold on with their hands and swing – none of which are designed for swinging – the beater on the permanent music structure, the rail on the den-making frame, the plastic strips in the doors! We are therefore making a bid for a small set of monkey bars and are awaiting a decision. Apart from monkey bars, the only other fixed equipment I would advocate are rope swings (with knots but without seats), trapeze rings and simple rope bridges. Unfortunately there are no trees on which we can hang ropes in this garden – trees are also on the wish list. One good argument for such equipment is that strong muscles in arms and shoulders in nursery will lead to better pencil control in year 1!

Setting up the environment

The mud kitchen

A close look at this photo explains how we have set up the mud kitchen. In September there was grass on the ground, but the combination of mud with water on grass was not very practical. The wood chip is a far better surface. I made the triangular shelving from long branches and old bits of decking – all drilled with small holes, through which cable ties have been used to secure the structure. It is also attached to the fence to stop it being pulled over.

I think that a simple battery powered screwdriver/drill is an essential piece of equipment for an early years practitioner. There are so many little tasks that can be done quickly and easily with this one tool.

Most of the utensils, pots and dishes are stored on the shelves permanently – no need to pack anything away. The digging area is just to the left – a source of the mud, which is combined with water, wood chip, grass, leaves, stones, etc. – to make wonderful soups, stews, curries and potions.

This wonderful pie was decorated with dandelions. It is far more educational to have regular discussions about which plants can be picked (weeds, some herbs, some leaves etc.) rather than a blanket rule that says not to pick anything. In this way the children are constantly enquiring and thinking about what is appropriate to use. Obviously there are still times when mistakes are made, but that is how we learn!

Setting up the environment

Outdoor construction

Real tools and jackets enhance the play and it then becomes more serious and thoughtful.

There are many examples of the construction area in use throughout the book – for example in the diary extract of Chapter 7: March. The large wooden blocks, from Community Playthings, are probably our most expensive resource, but well worth the investment, in terms of the learning opportunities that they offer. We are fortunate to have a sheltered area in the nursery garden and the blocks are stored on pallets under the shelter – always accessible to the children. In reception they are stored in a small shed – again always open and available to be used. However at a cost of nearly £2000, they are never used in the rain!

I have found several car bumpers (as seen at the top of this photo) at the side of the road. They are plastic, light weight and don't have sharp edges – perfect for early years!

We also have the following items available:

- Bread trays
- Milk crates
- Cable drums
- Car bumpers (found at the side of the road – these are light and safe for children to use)
- Steering wheels
- Number plates
- Planks
- Logs
- Rope
- Cones
- Wheelbarrows
- Car tyres
- Old booster seats
- Architects plans
- Other found items

Many of the items in this area have been found (beside bins, in skips, at the side of the road etc.) or donated (by parents, shops, staff).

On the shelf unit (see page 15) we have the tools that all good construction workers need, as well as 'high-vis' jackets and hard hats stored nearby.

Diary extracts: Examples of development and learning

WHAT TO LOOK OUT FOR

- Children settle back quickly after the Easter break.
- Many children demonstrate attention to detail in their pursuits.
- Many children are now able to work in partnership with a friend on a project.
- Some children are now showing an interest in 'writing'.

Snails

Today the children found holes in some of the leaves in the garden. They decided that an animal had eaten the leaves and remembered the Hungry Caterpillar. The group then decided to build a new house and collect some minibeasts to live there. The house was built but rather than caterpillars, all they could find were snails – lots and lots of snails. They concluded that perhaps the snails were eating the leaves.

Learning Journey For Muhammet... Term Summer Date 22.4.14

Entries should include the initial observation (& assessment), the teaching and the outcome.

		✓
COMMUNICATION AND LANGUAGE	P	✓
PHYSICAL DEVELOPMENT	R	✓
	I	
PERSONAL, SOCIAL AND EMOTIONAL DEVELOPMENT	M	✓
	E	
LITERACY	S	✓
MATHEMATICS	P	✓
UNDERSTANDING THE WORLD	C	
	E	
	C	✓
	I	
EXPRESSIVE ARTS AND DESIGN	F	✓
	C	
Obs indoors		
Obs outdoors		
Parent consultation		

Next Steps:
WPI - Counting - Mark Making
- books.

Identified Areas For Focus:
General/Parents: Stay focused for 5 mins on an activity.
Profile:
* Physical activities.
* Relationships with peers
* books

Muhammet played with two dinosaurs. ①Encouraged him to make a dinosaur ①modelled out of junk modelling. ①modelled language through out - teeth, foot, tail, etc. Muhammet repeated and roared. He attached an egg box to a box, then selected paint to paint a box. 'dinosaur.' ①encouraged him to put on an apron. 'help me please.' He painted the head... Another child picked up a pen and started to draw. Muhammet lost interest in painting and picked up a [drawing] to hold the pen correctly He drew circles using pen ①modelled how he was right hand.
Carterhatch

Muhammet joins another chd
Playing dinosaurs; happily takes two dinosaurs and joins in with peer. His friend with dinosaur. ①Explain he needs to be gentle Muhammet says 'sorry'
(continues to play with peer.

Muhammet joins in with chd threading Asks ① help him undo sorry while ① undoes string mentioned works off ①Encourages him to come back. Muhammet carries back M tries to thread a shape through gets a little frustrated ①modelled how to thread the shapes through Muhammet eventually does it on his own. very pleased with himself.
Stayed for 8 minutes

Muhammet playing with dinosaurs. 'I want big one' ① asks what he is going to make? walking dinosaur jump ① encourages him to make a house for the dinosaur He carefully puts blocks on top of each other ① encourages him to balance the bath walking at the top. He then stays at the activity for 5mins ① modelled language of shapes and positions throughout

Figure 8.1 Sample learning journey for April

Note: See Chapter 2: October for explanation.

In the moment planning – Nursery

W/C: 3.3.14   Term: Spring   Week: 9   Page: 2   Carterhatch

Focus Children:

* Hatun * Malachi * Maria * Melisa.

* Rayhan * Baran *   *

	PRIME AREAS			SPECIFIC AREAS			
	C&L	PHD	PSE	LIT	MATHS	UW	EXP A&D
	✓	✓	✓	✓	✓	✓	✓

Monday			Tuesday		Wednesday	Thursday	Friday
			✓				

	Observation and Assessment	(Plan and) Teaching	Outcome (Observation)
1:	Chn noticed the easel was very messy with paint	T encouraged chn to wash the easel – T provided soapywater and encouraged chn to use resources – sponges.	
2:	Chn tell me "We've got a new game to show you. Its Limbo."	Chn use slides to set up Limbo. T encouraged chn to change height of slide to make it more challenging.	Chn then show peers how to play Limbo.
3:	Chn mark making in sand.	T suggests to write names in sand. T modelues letters, then chd gover their names. T encourages chd to write their name on their own.	Some chd needed a little support to write name.
4:	Chn building a house.	T encouraged chn to look at Plans and notice details with in the house. They added a kitchen and toilet. T encouraged them to look at safety features when making stairs	Played for 2 hours house kept evolving in the end had a bedroom and car.
5:	chn sticking paper on the wall.	T encouraged chn to look at the logo on the wall and identify them. Also encouraged them to make their own	
6:	chn playing bear game.	T encouraged turn taking and for them to listen carefully to where the sound is coming from.	

Photo's

Figure 8.2 Sample 'Planning in the moment' sheet

After looking closely at the snails, one child decided to make a wooden snail and several others did the same. These were then placed in the bug hotel, and the real snails were returned there too.

Healthy teeth

Dila's pictures from home included this lovely photo of her brushing her teeth.

When this was shown on the interactive white board, it led to some discussion about how to keep teeth healthy and clean. It was clear that not all the children were in good habits and so Jacqui got in touch with the school nurse who came in to talk to the children. She brought a giant set of teeth, which led to further discussions and prompted some children to visit the dentist.

An interest in writing

The story scribing (see Chapter 4: December) is more popular than ever and many children are now attempting some writing of their own. Zipporah was delighted when her picture of the guinea pig, along with her writing of its name (Rosie), was attached to the cage for everyone to see.

The complete focus and desire to learn is seen in all the children – at whatever stage of development. A perfect example occurred today when Lewis spent the whole session working with his 'dragon'. He built it at the woodwork bench and then took it round the nursery to let it play. He took photos of the dragon at various points, for example riding a bike and reading a book.

He then watched as his photos were printed from the computer before he cut them out and stuck them on a sheet of paper. With encouragement, he dictated his 'story' and was keen to add his name as the author. He was delighted when his story was shared with the class during the group time at the end of the session.

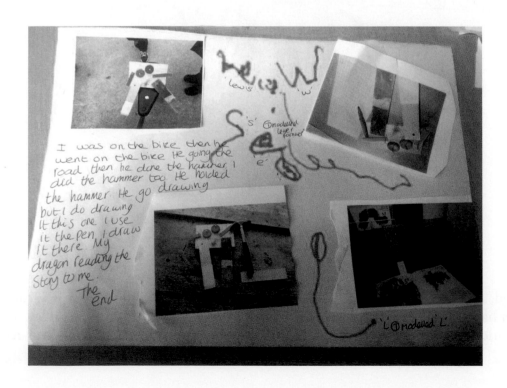

A few birthdays this week led to lots of talk about parties and role playing such events. One complete session was then spent organising a party – and of course invitations had to be written. In the picture below the children had gathered the name cards to be copied carefully so that no one was missed out. A list of food was then 'written' (and drawn) and a group went off to the shop to buy what was needed (on a very limited budget!). When time ran out, the party was delayed until the next day. The food was prepared, more cakes made, the children brought along their invitations and the party was a huge success. Writing was just another part of the game – making it more realistic and fun – not something to be avoided or feared.

Elvire was drawing and chatting away about her drawings – Jacqui took the opportunity to translate the spoken words and pictures into 'writing'. Each element of the 'story' can be seen in the pictures – even the 'cup of tea'!

As stated, April is a short month, in terms of the school days, but it is clear that the children have matured, settling quickly back into the routines after the holiday. Their play appears more 'serious' and complex, with many wonderful teaching moments for staff to exploit.

9 May

May is the month when we are forced to start thinking about transitions – both into and out of nursery and I explain some of the work involved. In this chapter I have combined the environment section with the diary section, looking in detail at the growing area. This includes a month-by-month guide as to how to develop such an area over the course of a year, covering the organisation and resources, as well as the events that happen.

MAY: TO DO LIST
- Continue with third and final cycle of focus children.
- Continue with third and final cycle of parent meetings.
- Start to arrange the children into groups for reception (if you are a school-based nursery).
- Contact other schools if children are transferring to other settings.
- Make contact with new families and arrange visit sessions.

Transitions

As mentioned in Chapter 1: September, transitions are very stressful for young children and need to be handled with great care and planning. The children in nursery will be moving into reception classes in September and parents will have been told which school their children are going to. In addition, the new cohort of nursery children will also have been offered places at nursery and we need to start making links with these families as soon as possible.

When a nursery is attached to a school, then the organisation of transition is far simpler for the children who are staying at the school and this year that is the vast majority of our children. The staff look carefully at each child to decide which other children they should be grouped with in one of our three reception classes. Once this is decided then we start to take groups of children into the reception area to play in their new classroom and garden (these visits start in June and continue through July). By the end of the year, they will be totally familiar with the layout, the routines and the staff. The reception teachers also spend some of their PPA time visiting the nursery to see the children in that environment too. Some children are transferring to other schools and we ensure that we contact those schools and invite the teachers to visit the nursery too. We also organise meetings for parents, to explain the transition process and to clarify what will happen at the start of the reception year. Towards the end of the year (in July), we organise an open evening when the children can attend with their parents. During the evening they can play in the reception area, show their parents around, spend time with their teacher, buy uniform and ask questions. We also give each child a laminated card to take home (see photo below). This is something to look at during the long summer holiday so that they remember who their teacher will be, which class they will be in and what the class looks like.

For the new nursery children, we write to all the families, inviting them to visit the nursery. We allocate visits of about an hour for up to four families at a time (these visits will happen during June and July). During the visit the children can play in the nursery, get used to the layout and meet the staff (if staff have been finalised by this point!). Parents can meet other families as well as the staff, ask questions and begin to support their children to learn the routines and expectations of the nursery. The most important outcome of the visit is that the child enjoys nursery and is keen to return in September! We also need to allocate morning or afternoon places for September and parents complete a form to say which sessions they would prefer and to give reasons for their choice.

Setting up the environment and diary

The growing area

WHAT TO LOOK OUT FOR
- Children start to talk about their new school.
- Children feel positive about the transition.
- New nursery families request visits.

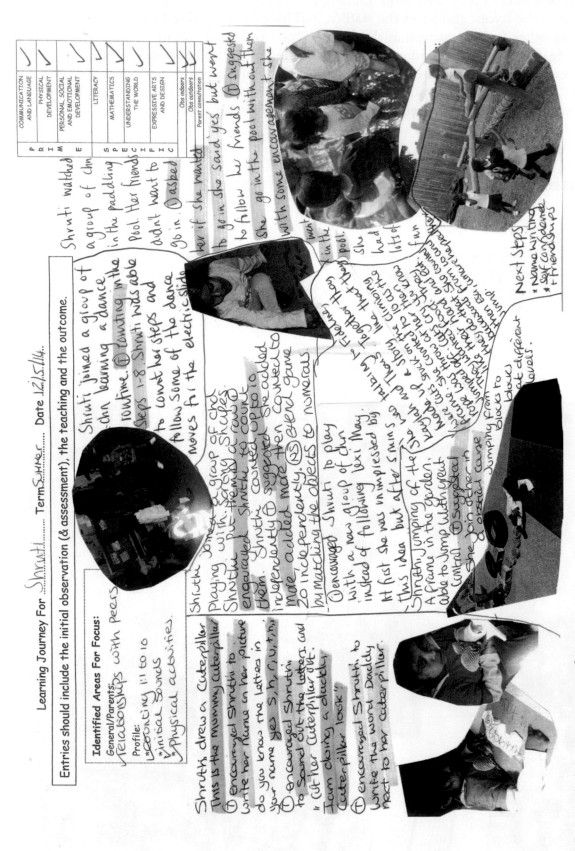

Figure 9.1 Sample learning journey for May

Note: See Chapter 2: October for explanation.

Many settings struggle to have a successful growing area and I think the biggest tip I would give is to involve the children and to do the work during session times. If you try to do the tasks outside of sessions, you will probably give up. This year the children have built the growing beds, moved a tonne of soil into place, planted seeds into pots and transferred them to the beds, watered, weeded and harvested. When jobs needed doing, the children who were interested became involved and gained valuable skills and knowledge as they worked. Figure 9.2 gives a rough guide as to the tasks that were completed in each month. If you plan to try and start a growing area, then make use of the Internet to research – and involve the children at that stage too. Figure 9.2 is not meant to be a definite plan – each year will differ according to the weather – but the main message is to have a go!

Month, tasks and comments	Photos and comments
September Select an area to develop (if the area is concrete, then you will need deeper soil on top of the concrete). Order soil and seeds. Find or request logs (from your local parks department). Use two layers of sleepers if you have a concrete base. Dig up grass or bushes. Place logs or sleepers as the boundary. Fill area with soil.	 We chose to develop a flower bed and strip of grass.  The children spent many hours moving 1 tonne of soil into place.

Month, tasks and comments	Photos and comments
October Add access paths (decking or stepping stones are fine). Add trellis and/or sticks to support tall plants. Fix tools nearby (on the fence in this photo). At this stage it was fine for the children to walk on the soil and dig it over. Once the plants are in, then new rules will be discussed and agreed.	
November and December Plant fruit trees (if you plan to have these). Plant garlic. These children are digging holes for the grape vines to go into. They also planted several garlic cloves and were watering them when the OFSTED inspector arrived. Herbs can be planted at any time during the year.	

Month, tasks and comments	Photos and comments
January Plant fruit bushes – strawberries, raspberries etc. If the children can be involved in buying the seeds, then even better. We are lucky to have a shop near to school. Plant broad beans in pots outside.	 Alfie is examining the strawberry plants.  

Month, tasks and comments	Photos and comments
February If mild, plant carrots, parsnips, onions, lettuces and radishes. Put the beans from the pots into the soil. The canes are pushed into the ground for the beans to climb up – lots of measuring possibilities here.	 
March Plant cabbages and leeks.	

Month, tasks and comments	Photos and comments
April Put straw around strawberry plants. Sow seeds in pots such as marrows, courgettes, tomatoes and cucumbers. Plant potatoes – these are best grown in big bags (see July photo). A mention in our newsletter resulted in several plants being donated and these could be planted outdoors in May (avoiding the need to plant seeds in pots).	
May Move the plants from the pots to outside or buy (or be given) established plants. Plant sweetcorn. A few items might be ready to pick e.g. herbs, lettuce, etc. Support tall bushes with canes and ties. Snails were in abundance this year – very annoying for the plants, but great for conversations and investigations.	 

Month, tasks and comments	Photos and comments
June Water, water, water. Water from a water butt is the best for the plants.	
July Harvest as much as possible before the children leave for the summer break. Some produce will be ready when the new children arrive in September. Allow the children to taste as much of the produce as possible. Vegetable soup is easy and lots of children will be interested in getting involved. Raspberries!	 

Month, tasks and comments	Photos and comments
The potatoes are being harvested in this photo.	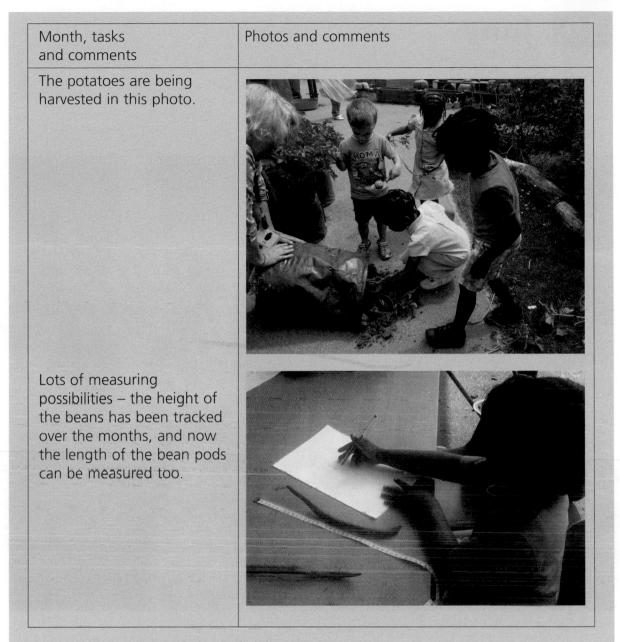
Lots of measuring possibilities – the height of the beans has been tracked over the months, and now the length of the bean pods can be measured too.	

Figure 9.2 Calendar of events for the growing area

As the month of May comes to an end, we have one final break before the last half term in school. We have made initial contact with new families, but have yet to meet very many of them. The nursery children are beginning to talk about reception and it is great that they feel so positive about the move. The transition work will now continue until the end of the year, ensuring that the children's confidence and 'can-do' disposition, which the staff have worked so hard to develop, will be maintained.

10 June

While May was the month for organising transition events, June is when the bulk of these events occur. It is vital that, however stressed the staff are feeling, the children remain secure and confident – thus able to continue to learn and develop. With so many visits from nursery to reception and visitors to nursery, it is at this time that we appreciate just how independent the children have become. Most of them take these new events in their stride, indeed they relish the new experiences and challenges. The visiting families comment on how calm and independent the nursery children appear and many express delight at the nursery environment and the opportunities that it offers. In this chapter, I review the curriculum coverage; in the environment section I look at the resources in the carpet areas; and in the diary section I give some examples to demonstrate how children thrive when they are secure within set boundaries – using examples from the carpet area. I also briefly look at the mystery of snail pooh!

JUNE: TO DO LIST

- Continue final cycle of focus children.
- Continue final cycle of parent meetings.
- Begin transition records for children transferring to a different school.
- Begin transition visits to the reception classes.
- Meet with new families when they come to visit nursery.
- Flag up any issues that arise regarding new families.
- Review the year and decide on changes for the new year.
- Organise home visit timetable for September.

Reviewing practice

June is the perfect time to reflect on the year and decide if you want to make any changes in the next academic year. If you are thinking about making dramatic changes to your practice, you need to think carefully about the timing of such changes. Young children thrive in predictable routines and need changes to be made gradually. Therefore, if you do make changes during the year, these should be small changes. Larger, more fundamental changes should be introduced with the new cohort of children from day one – new group, new routines.

Curriculum coverage

I am often asked how we ensure that the whole curriculum is covered if we don't plan ahead. My answer is that we monitor the children carefully and in light of this we discuss and review the environment, the organisation, the staff and the routines on a regular basis. We make amendments to ensure our environment remains outstanding. The staff are trained and coached so that they are outstanding too. Therefore (as OFSTED recognised) the curriculum is covered and the children make outstanding progress in all areas.

The Creative Cascade set is used in many different ways by the children throughout the year. Indeed all areas of learning can be covered with this challenging, flexible equipment.

Individuals

The staff know the children very well and will know if a child is not accessing a particular area of learning (this is in fact very rare) or not making expected progress. They will usually know why this is the case too. If we are not sure of the reasons, we will assess the child over a period of a day or a week, using the levels of involvement (and if necessary the levels of well-being) to try and see a pattern and triggers to their behaviour. Discussions among the team might lead to the introduction of a new resource or routine. Sometimes we might have a meeting with parents and also an outside agency might be called in. As stated, every child has a natural desire to learn and this is the basis for all our work. We have to find a way to tap into that desire or find out if there is a problem, an anxiety or a stress that is preventing that natural state from being sustained. A detailed look at such work is beyond the scope of this book, but I would stress that if a child is not getting deeply involved in their learning (in spite of a superb environment and fantastic staff), then seek outside help and advice.

In recent years I have dealt with all of the following issues or needs and in each case the approach and solution were different (and in some cases, unfortunately, we were not able to resolve the issue): specific learning difficulties (e.g. autism, dyslexia, dyspraxia etc.), attachment disorder, global delay, abuse (physical, sexual, emotional), parents with alcohol/drug dependency, extreme poverty, various phobias, speech impediment, selective mutism, physical disability, illness, ill parent, genetic disorder, violence at home, lack of sleep, screen addiction/over-use, forced formal learning at home, poor diet, poor parenting (e.g. lack of boundaries), trauma (from war etc.), temporary housing, absent parents, etc. The list is endless. As teachers it is estimated that we can only impact on 20 per cent of the attainment of any child – 80 per cent is dependent on other factors. That is not to say we should give up – rather we have to do the best we can to ensure our 20 per cent has maximum impact. However, it is important to recognise outside factors and to rectify, improve or mitigate their impact where possible.

Cohort

On occasions, in the past, when staff have said that they are not seeing much evidence of learning in a particular area (for a lot of the children), then we have amended the provision or the organisation to ensure coverage. This was why (several years ago) we started using cameras for the children to take home. At that time, we were finding it difficult to get the children to talk freely about their family life. As soon as there were photos to refer to, this became much easier. Similarly, when we were struggling with some aspects of the understanding of the world, we made a determined effort to develop the permanent investigation unit and the growing area, and this ensured coverage easily. Story scribing (see Chapter 4: December) is the most important aspect of our work in terms of developing literacy. It is also such fun and therefore a pleasure to pursue, as opposed to several other literary pursuits that we have tried – many of which have felt like a chore both for the staff and the children. Regular cooking activities are a natural extension of children's play and these have ensured much maths coverage. Numicon, too, has led to coverage of more number concepts as children play – for example in the mud and sand etc. (rather than forced maths activities). As mentioned, at present we have noticed a need for somewhere for the children to swing from and we are therefore pursuing the addition of some monkey bars and rope swings to the nursery garden. The reception area is lucky to have a tree on which we can hang ropes and trapeze rings.

Setting up the environment

Carpet areas

Our nursery room caters for up to 46 children and although it is essentially one large space, we have ensured that there are two carpet areas so that the children can be split for group times and also to create two separate areas at other times.

The photo below shows the largest carpet and the interactive white board is visible in this area. As explained, in Chapter 4: December, the group times are at the end of the sessions (morning and afternoon) and are used for songs, stories, games, acting stories and showing photos etc. At other times this carpet is used for numerous activities for which the resources are stored around the edge of the carpet. As the photo shows, the storage units serve the extra purpose of creating a protective barrier around the carpet. This helps to prevent children walking across the carpet (and possibly spoiling a wonderful creation) and it helps to keep the resources contained within the area. In addition, at home time, it helps to contain the children until their parents arrive. There are just two 'exit' points from the carpet so that it is easy for staff to monitor who is leaving the carpet area to go to a parent.

The resources around the edge are listed below, but this is by no means an exhaustive list of possibilities. The white unit near the window is from Ikea – very reasonably priced and very sturdy. Other units appear in photos throughout the book. Resources include:

I often visit settings where the carpet area is only used at group times and is empty for the rest of the session. In such settings, the construction toys etc. are stored and used elsewhere, usually in a small space in another part of the room. It makes much more sense to store resources around the carpet as shown here, so that the space is in use for as much of the session as possible.

- Construction toys (Duplo, small Lego, community blocks (small and mini sets), coloured shaped blocks;
- Wooden train set;
- Cars and other vehicles, car park, road way;
- Large wooden vehicles – aeroplane, helicopter, trucks, tractors, boat, diggers;
- People;
- Numicon;
- Books – reference and fiction;
- Animals – sorted into various baskets – dinosaurs, wild animals, farm animals;
- Natural resources – stones, pinecones, sticks, shells etc.;
- Variety of fabric pieces;
- Abacus;
- Electronic toys;
- Nesting dolls;
- Puzzles, games, threading toys, stacking toys etc.;
- Unit containing individual folders.

Clearly this list invites an infinite variety of activities. However, we review the area and will add or remove resources if levels of involvement drop. We also insist that children tidy away the resources that they have been using before they leave the carpet. In this way it remains inviting for others.

Figure 1.3 of Chapter 1: September, shows our plan of the class, with the second carpet area at the other end of the room and it is seen in the photo below. This is where the main book area is (including story props and puppets), a sofa, the 'pop-up' role-play area, a storage unit for some individual folders and the guinea pig cage.

Diary extracts: Examples of development and learning

WHAT TO LOOK OUT FOR

- Children talking about moving into reception classes.
- New families visit the nursery.
- Staff from other settings visit the nursery.
- Children become more confident when visiting the reception classes.
- Children bring further complexity and depth to activities.

Examples from the carpet areas

In many of these examples, we see complexity that would not often be associated with such young children. It is possible in this nursery in the carpet areas because the carpets are large, protected (i.e. they are not walkways) and well resourced (with a good quantity and variety of open-ended, quality resources). Also the children have learnt that they can

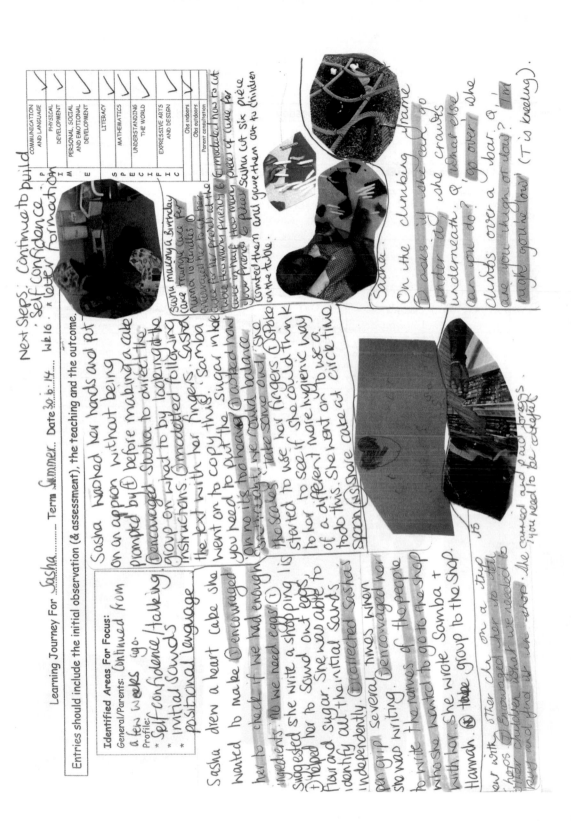

Figure 10.1 Sample learning journey for June

Note: See Chapter 2: October for explanation.

In the moment planning - Nursery

W/C: 12.5.14   Term: Summer   Week: 4   Page: 2

Carterhatch

Focus Children:

*   *   *   *

*   *   *   *

PRIME AREAS			SPECIFIC AREAS			
C&L	PHD	PSE	LIT	MATHS	UW	EXP A&D
✓	✓	✓	✓	✓	✓	✓

Monday		Tuesday	Wednesday	Thursday	Friday

	Observation and Assessment	(Plan and) Teaching	Outcome (Observation)
1:	Chn finding snails and putting them in water.	ⓣ Spoke to chn about snails not being able to swim ⓣ suggested they make the snails a house and find them food to eat,	Made snails houses on woodwork bench
2:	Chn looking at beans growing up stalks.	Chn guessing how far they would grow in 1 day. ⓣ provided sticker for them to mark poles to monitor growth.	
3:	Chn interested in making witches hats + wands.	ⓣ modelled how to make the hats & Chn decide to stick them together with sticky tape. ⓣ provided resources for wands + models how to make	then. Chn then decide on the magic words they will use.
4:	Chn wanted to know where snails mouth was.	ⓣ Put snail on door so they could see underneath it	Children observed how snail moved + mouth parts
5:	Chn running around screaming	ⓣ Suggested they play what's the time Mr Wolf' - chn counting out, taking turns to be first.	
6:	Chn complaining that it was hot.	ⓣ spoke to chn about ways to cool down. They decided to they wanted a paddling pool.	- Took off own shoes and put them on. - Followed ⓣ instruction - no jumping / runn in the water.

Photo's

Figure 10.2 Sample 'Planning in the moment' sheet

take risks and that their efforts will be recognised; they know that adults will support them if necessary; they are clear about the rules and boundaries so that, within those rules, they can experiment and combine resources as they wish; they know that other children will not disrupt their play; and finally they know that they have as much time as they need to create even the most complex models. In each of the examples below, the creation was photographed and the photo annotated for the child's folder. In some cases, the adult spent time discussing the model with the child to find out the child's intention and reasoning. In many settings, adults are relieved when children are 'occupied' with construction toys etc. so that they can get on with focus tasks. I would urge such adults to spend a day on the carpet, protecting the work that the children are doing so that their ideas are brought into reality – remember if they are deeply involved, their brains are 'lit up' and they are learning. If you want to know exactly what they are learning, you need to join them and observe carefully.

In the photo above we can see Melissa interacting with Osuani, not to interrogate or assess him, but purely out of curiosity and a desire to support his learning. She is not holding a clip board or pen, she is right down at the child's level and she discovered that Osuani was actually making a bus station, sticking to the exact layout of the bus station that he was familiar with from his journeys to school.

At first glance, the arrangement of blocks above may seem random. However the annotation of this photo means that the true value of this play is revealed. Such information is acquired because the adults are free to observe, skilled at doing so and really want to discover what is in a child's mind as they play. In this instance there is a house, a school and a funfair, along with specific contents in each location and routes to and from each area.

Zipporah spent nearly an hour creating this line of two-storey blocks, with level 5 involvement throughout the process. Learning possibilities include concepts of width, height, length, shape, balance, order, resilience, perseverance, concentration, pride, etc. She might be interested in counting the blocks, but I very much doubt it and she might be making something specific – again I doubt it. The only way to be sure is to join the activity and ponder – i.e. say 'I wonder what this is?...' But don't worry if there is no response – the learning is happening through the process, whether or not the child articulates it.

As explained above, Ronaz needed enough blocks, as well as space, time and confidence even to attempt this structure. She also needed to know that no-one would knock it over half way through.

Another storage unit is visible at the top of this photo. The resources in this unit are in transparent boxes, labelled with photo and word, so that even if they are completely emptied, the children will be able to return the resources to the correct box.

In this example Shruthi and Kayra worked together over a long period to create this masterpiece, combining resources from several different boxes. It is fascinating to note that in this instance when an adult joined the girls on the carpet and pondered about their creation, it was as if the spell had been broken – they packed it all away and went outside! Deep-level learning had been happening, but we are not always successful in discovering what that learning is. However, it doesn't mean that the learning didn't happen; it did and it will be applied in situations in the future.

Resources have been combined here too – blocks, fabric and people – to create a hospital.

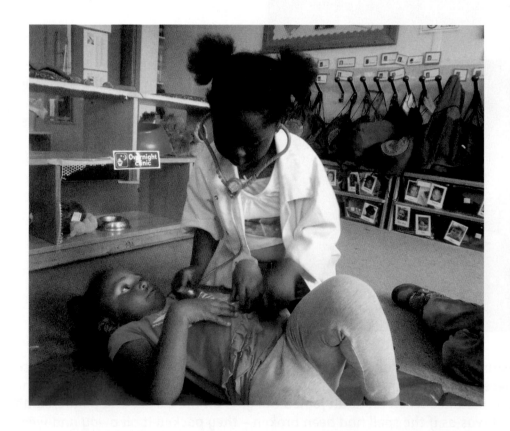

On the smaller carpet area, the vet's surgery, which has been set up for a couple of weeks, is often used as a doctor's again. Children play what they are familiar with and not many have any experience of visiting a vet!

The mystery of the pooh!

The abundance of snails continues to fascinate the children. This group noticed the snail had done a pooh! 'But where is its bottom?' was the question they wanted to answer. The magnifying glass did not provide any new information and the reference books did not help either. Jacqui suggested they should look under the snails and she provided them with a sheet of clear Perspex (from a display board). When this got too heavy to hold, the group built some walls to hold the Perspex and they were then able to crawl underneath and look up at the snails.

So what did they discover about snail pooh? One question for you to find the answer to yourself!

As June comes to an end, it is striking how the children are thriving — growing in confidence and ambition — and it is easy to take their disposition for granted. However it has not happened without a lot of hard work from the staff. I deliver a lot of training and one message that is often missed or misheard regards boundaries. I do advocate allowing children to have the freedom to pursue their own interests but that freedom is limited by definite boundaries that are enforced consistently. Young children thrive when they feel safe. They do not feel safe in chaos or in an environment where there are no rules or boundaries. Some children will test such boundaries over and over again, which can be exhausting for the adults. However, it is these children who actually need and want the boundaries more than many others. They are often vulnerable children who may be living in chaos and want reassurance that nursery is different. Although it may appear that they want the boundaries to shift, that is in fact the last thing they want – they want to know that the boundaries are firm, that the adults are in charge and that they can therefore get on with being a child. It is in that atmosphere that children can relax, explore, take risks and learn, as the examples in this book show.

11 July

The final month of the school year is always stressful for the staff. They continue to meet the needs of the current cohort, finalise assessments, write reports and transition records (if needed) and meet with reception staff. They are also beginning to plan for the new group of children who will start in September – flagging up any additional needs that they have noticed, ensuring new stock is ordered, arranging for any large-scale work to be done over the holiday period, reviewing the environment and making changes. In this chapter, I give the final data summary, and explain how we do reports and how these are linked to the characteristics of effective learning. I also look briefly at one area of the environment that we are proposing to change. The remainder of the chapter is given over to numerous examples of effective learning that were observed this month.

JULY: TO DO LIST

- Finish final cycle of focus children.
- Finish final cycle of parent meetings.
- Write a report for each child.
- Finalise assessments for each child for the end of year.
- Finalise transition records for children transferring to a different school.
- Continue with transition visits to the Reception classes
- Meet with reception teachers to share information about the children.
- Meet with new families when they come to visit nursery.
- Flag up any issues that arise regarding new families.
- Carry out a stock check and place orders for resources.

Final data

The data summary in Figure 11.1 shows clearly the progress that the cohort has made. At the start of the year 80 per cent of the children were below, or well below, their expected levels. By the end of the year this figure had dropped to 42 per cent. At the start of the year 20 per cent were working at, or above, the expected level. By the end of the year, this figure had risen to 58 per cent. In order for the data to be truly reflective, and as accurate as possible, the summary is based on the prime areas.

Nursery	% well below expected level	% below expected level	% at expected level	% above expected level
Entry September 2013	37	43	15	5
Term 1 December 2013	22	42	31	5
Term 2 March 2014	18	34	41	7
Term 3 July 2014	7	35	51	7

Figure 11.1 Final data for OFSTED

I stress again, however, that there is no statutory requirement to gather data in this format (or any other). If OFSTED visit, they want to see that you have systems in place to check that all children are making progress, but they do not specify how you go about this. The grid in Figure 11.1 is a useful snapshot in some respects, but it is worthless in terms of telling us anything about any individual child. The individual folders and the wealth of knowledge that the staff hold in their heads are far more valuable in terms of telling the story of an individual child.

The data also fail to reflect the even more dramatic progress that has been made in PSE, with nearly 90 per cent of the children operating at or above expected levels by the end of the year. Figure 11.2 shows the data for PSE only for entry and term three.

Nursery – PSE data only	% well below expected level	% below expected level	% at expected level	% above expected level
Entry September 2013	27	50	18	5
Term 3 July 2014	5	9	68	18

Figure 11.2 PSE data for entry and term three

For me, these PSE data demonstrate that the nursery has been successful. These children are leaving nursery with the confidence, independence and positive attitude that will allow them to achieve their full potential in years to come.

Reviewing the environment

As mentioned, we have an ongoing wish list and one area that we have wanted to develop is the large expanse of concrete in one section of the garden. As I write this chapter this wish has come true! We have gathered logs and four cubic metres of bark have been delivered to nursery. This has transformed the hard, dull, grey surface to something far more inviting and warm. The two pictures below show the initial transformation. The PE equipment and large blocks will be used in this area – which now has a permanent soft surface – protecting the children and the blocks from damage!

Reports

We have a statutory requirement to report to parents at the end of the year. Again, however, the format and content are largely left to our discretion. Our head teacher recognises that the children's folders document their learning and development over the course of the year. This year we decided to make sure that the parents understood that the folder was the source of all the information about their child. Anything extra contained in a report is a tiny supplement. Therefore the reports this year consisted of one A4 page for each child as set out below.

The teacher scribed some comments from the child in the box on the right and the child added a drawing. The attendance was noted in the box in the lower right-hand corner. The reports were very concise, but truly unique to each child. They were handed to the parent in nursery when they were able to look at the folder if they wished. The parents also knew that they would be able to take the folder home at the end of the year.

Celebration of

Achievement of

Kiara

Nursery 2013 – 2014

Kiara's folder and learning journeys are a record of all the wonderful learning from the time spent in Nursery.

The characteristics of effective learning are:- playing and exploring, active learning and creating and thinking critically.

One example of learning effectively was;

Kiara is becoming more confident when arriving at nursery and leaving her mum. She quickly finds her friend and they spend all afternoon together. Kiara enjoys creative activities and was observed in the creative area folding and sticking a piece of paper. Kiara folded the top of the paper into a triangle. Kiara turned to her friend and said, 'I am making a house, this is the roof' as she points to the triangle. Kiara then finds a pen. She starts to draw figures with arms and legs, 'that's me, my daddy; I got my mummy in the house. I play pushchair at home'. Her friend tells her teenagers don't have children. Kiara replies, 'you're absolutely right'. She returns to her drawing, 'this is my daddy's bed, my brother's bed and this one is my bed. This is my room with my sister'.

At nursery, I like to

"play outside, playing with Hatun in the sand pit"

Attendance

Excellent, keep it up ☑

Improvement needed ☐

Serious concerns;
Attendance must improve ☐

The characteristics of effective learning

As I have stressed before, *Development Matters* is not a statutory document — we are under no obligation to use it. However, there is much useful information contained within it, not least the sections referring to the characteristics of effective learning. These characteristics are also referred to in the current statutory framework for the EYFS, which states:

> Three characteristics of effective teaching and learning are:
>
> - **playing and exploring** — children investigate and experience things, and 'have a go';
> - **active learning** — children concentrate and keep on trying if they encounter difficulties, and enjoy achievements; and
> - **creating and thinking critically** — children have and develop their own ideas, make links between ideas, and develop strategies for doing things.
>
> (DfES, 21014: 12)

I hope, if you have read the whole of this book, that it is evident that the pedagogy I am following allows children to learn effectively all the time — each day from the moment they arrive in nursery (or reception) until the moment they leave. To conclude this chapter I have selected some examples from the reports that were written by Jacqui this month. They represent a selection of activities that happened in nursery in July and they are all examples of the children learning effectively.

Diary extracts: Examples of effective learning

Melisa moves a variety of resources into the tepee with her friend. She sets up a cot using a community block. Melisa finds stones and takes them back to the tepee where she uses them as food for the baby. Melisa tells her friend, 'You sister, I the mum, that the dog and that the baby'. She then says to her friend, 'Ok sister you go sleep ok'. She selects a book opens it and uses picture cues to tell the story. 'Baby is doing eating, yuk! Stinky'.

Demar uses a small bucket to fill up sand moulds. He tells his friends 'I'm making cakes. I'm going to put them in the oven'. He then lines the moulds up on the edge of the sand pit, where other children join him. He speaks to his friends and tells them, 'You need to make more cakes'. Demar then counts his cakes, '1, 2, 3, 4, 5, I got five. Let me count yours'. He counts all the cakes up to eight. 'We need to make fish cakes now'. Demar fills the balance buckets with sand and directs his friends to help. 'We need more, I'm ready now'. He transfers the sand into bowls: 'Now let's put that in the oven'. Demar sits down and counts them '1, 2, 3, 4, 5, 6, 7, 8, 9, 10 that's how much. They gonna be hot on your hands so I'll put them in the freezer to be cold so I can eat it'.

Sasha plays at the playdough table making cakes. She asks a teacher if she can make a real cake. The teacher supplies her with resources and leaves Sasha and her friends to make a cake independently. Sasha takes the lead. Looking at the recipe book, she gives her friends instructions on how to make the cake. Sasha's friend puts too much sugar in the scales: 'You need to take some out'. She looks at the next picture: 'We need butter'. Sasha finds two spoons and carefully puts the butter in the scales. She then transfers it into the bowl. At the mixing stage, Sasha says 'Everyone can have a turn'. She moves the bowl around her friends. When it is her turn she says, 'It's hard to mix ... it's ready ... the lumps are gone'. She then pours it into a baking tray and passes it over to an adult: 'Can you put it in the oven please'.

Ryan and his friends find their special books in the class. Ryan sits next to his friends and they start to look at the photos in their folders: 'Look that's me outside. Kayra has her coat on'. He listens to his friends talking about their pictures and makes relevant comments. 'Look at that – what are you doing?'. The conversation leads on to what they like doing at nursery. Ryan says, 'I like eating when I'm hungry, running, riding the bikes and reading stories'. Ryan becomes very excited at one of the pages in his book: 'Look at my writing', he tells his friends.

Maria is outside in the nursery garden and looks in the bushes for stones. She fills a bucket with stones and then notices a child filling a box with water. She becomes fascinated by this and wants to put water in with her stones. She finds a bottle and starts to fill the bucket with water; she fills it to the top. Maria carefully carries it to the two-seater bike and places it on the shelf underneath the seats. She calls over to her friend: 'You want to ride on my bike? I am going to India'. She talks to her friend about the stones under her seat: 'My stones are so shiny because I put water on it'. She then stops the bike, retrieves the bucket and goes up to her peers showing them the stones: 'Look so shiny'.

Alfie watches the teacher watering the vegetable patch with a hose. Alfie goes off and selects a plastic tube with a pump and a bucket. He speaks to his friend and encourages her to fill the bucket with water and hold it while he puts the plastic tube in it: 'Look, I made my own hose'. Alfie squeezes the pump and begins to water the plants. He talks with his friend about why the plants need water. Alfie notices some tomatoes growing: 'Look tomatoes, they're green, they need to grow a really long time, then they will turn red'. His friend asks for a turn with the hose: 'Oh I had it first. Is it your turn?'. He hands over the hose and takes his turn at filling the bucket with water.

Adelle is in the creative area with her friends. She selects resources and starts to draw a picture: 'That's me, that's the bread, that's the small mountains'. Adelle writes her name from memory using recognisable letters. She finds some wool and sticks a piece onto her picture: 'It's a kite'. Her friends adapt their pictures to be kites too. 'We need cold and windy weather now'. Adelle takes her kite outside with her friends following. They start to run around the climbing frame singing as they run. The wool keeps coming away from the paper. Adelle tries to re-stick it several times. 'I think I need a plaster, that will fix it'. The teacher provides her with a plaster and she sticks it on to her kite and runs around the climbing frame: 'It worked!'. Adelle notices that her friend's string is coming loose: 'You need a plaster as well. It really works you know'.

Muhammet is playing with the Duplo. He selects a base board and looks through the Duplo box choosing small blocks. He checks every block before placing it onto the base board, filling most of the board. Muhammet has one gap on the board; he looks for a small block to fit in the gap. Unable to find one, he finds a longer block and places it in the space. Not happy with his design, he reworks the blocks and places two blocks on top so they both stick out at the sides. Happy with his model he stands up and starts to fly it around the carpet. Muhammet shows everyone his plane.

Hannah plays in the water tray with her friend. They make the babies jump up and down in the water: 'This is pretend mud. We need to wash our baby's hair because they're all dirty. I'm getting a sponge'. Hannah gets a sponge for her friend too and they both start singing, 'under the sea, under the sea'. Hannah then washes the baby clothes and hangs them up: 'I'm hanging up my baby clothes. They need to get dry. 1, 2, 3, 4, 5, 6, 7, 8 yep 8. I'm washing all of them'. Her friend begins to talk about her family and Hannah says 'My mum washes my hair and sometimes we have a shower by ourselves, but not all the time. When I'm a grown up I will'.

Michael plays outside with the community blocks. He helps build a car with another child. He selects blocks and tyres then finds a hammer and starts to knock the pieces together: 'Bang, bang, I got my ear muffs'. When he has finished he sits inside the tyre and says to his friend, 'I have ear muffs so I can listen to music'. Michael then starts to hum. Later he says, 'I got a bag of screws. We're moving house. You need to go to a different house because someone else wants to move in'. Michael then starts to move the blocks, stacking them carefully on top of each other to build a house.

Amira sits at the creative table, sticking tape onto a piece of paper: 'It's all sticky'. Amira continues to stick tape on the paper. When she can't cut the tape with the dispenser, she finds some scissors and cuts it with these. Amira tells someone on the table, 'I'm making a rainbow, some butterflies and wiggly worms for the birds to eat'. She puts more tape onto her picture: 'This is a long wiggly worm'. Amira then selects different coloured paint and paints a rainbow and sun on her picture. She mixes paint: 'Look an orange on the floor, I mixed yellow and red'. She then makes green: 'This is the grass'. Amira adds her name to the picture.

Harley plays on the carpet arranging wooden blocks to make a house for the animals. She speaks to her friend throughout explaining her choices in the arrangement of the blocks. 'Rose, Tulip and Rosie need a house, otherwise they will run away. I need to decorate with these circles'. Harley then selects long flat blocks and places them on top of her house: 'That's to stop the rain from getting in'. She uses crescent shapes in the centre of one of the rooms: 'I'm using these so baby can look at them'.

Zinar plays in the outdoor area with friends, using the hand and feet supports to climb the wall. Zinar reaches the top of the fence. He is able to support his body weight for a few moments before dropping down. He repeats this several times. His friends speak to him in Turkish and try their hardest to copy him. Zinar then uses his hands and feet to move his body along the wall. He concentrates and perseveres until he masters this skill. When he gets to the other end of the wall he drops down and smiles to his friends and begins speaking to them in Turkish.

Thais plays in the paddling pool with her peers. She finds a net and starts to catch the plastic fish. Thais says to her friend, 'Look I've got two'. Her friend says 'I caught more'. Thais starts to count the fish in her friend's net: 'You have four, so I have more'. Her friend disagrees and Thais says, 'Let's count again'. Thais then puts more fish in her net and counts correctly: 'I have five, you have four. I have more'. Her friend starts to put the fish from her net into Thais' net. Thais said 'You have none, I mean zero. I've got more'. Thais tipped all the fish in the water. 'Let's catch them again. Ready steady go!'.

Kayra makes a cake in the mud kitchen. She works with a group of friends to mix water and mud together until it is 'thick and sticky'. She transfers the mixture into several pots and bowls: 'We need candles'. She goes inside and comes out with some candles: 'Oh no we only have three. Who is three?'. The group talks for a while about their ages. Kayra then goes back inside and comes out with another candle: 'There you go. We have four now'. A friend starts to decorate the cake with flowers. Kayra starts to arrange the flowers on the top: 'I think you have put enough on now. I'll put it in the oven'. After it is cooked Kayra sings Happy Birthday and says 'hip hip hooray'; 'Right who wants some cake?'. She then cuts it into slices and puts it on plates, making sure all of her friends have a piece.

Rayhan plays in the outdoor area with his friend, 'Come on, come. Let's go'. His friend asks for help to put his walkie-talkie in his pocket. Rayhan immediately begins to help: 'There you go'. He then runs off and makes a walkie-talkie out of card. He shows his friend: 'Look – this is my one. It shoots bang, bang'. They run around the garden using their walkie-talkies. 'Look an insect. It looks like an ant'. His friend suggests that it's a cockroach: 'Yeah it's an ant, cockroach, and insect'. 'Oh no! He's gonna get stuck. Look he can climb up the blocks'. Rayhan is so excited and picks up the flying ant. 'I'm going to look after him'. He suggests they make the insect a house and his friend agrees. Rayhan places the flying ant on the blocks and helps to finish off the house: 'These are the walls. Let's use all of the blocks. We need a ball for him to play with'.

Muhammed joins a group digging up the potatoes. He uses the garden spade to break the soil apart in search of potatoes: 'Look – 1, 2, 3, 4, 5'. Throughout he speaks to his friend in Turkish. When they come across a worm, Muhammed holds it up in the air: 'Snake'. His friend tells him it's a worm and Muhammed repeats 'Worm', as he shows all the children around him. He goes on to find more worms, adding each one to a pile next to him. His peers start to take an interest in the pile and Muhammed separates them and counts them in sequence: 'Ten!'.

Guiseppe is at the woodwork bench. He uses a hammer and nails two pieces of wood together: 'I'm making an aeroplane', he tells his friend opposite him. He speaks to his friend throughout: 'Do you like my ironman t-shirt?'. He checks to see if the nail is secure in the two pieces of wood that he is trying hard to connect. It is not secure so he continues to hammer, saying 'Bang, bang, bang'. Once this is done he says 'It's going on an adventure, I'm going to draw batman'. He finds a pen and starts to draw a face: 'Ironman's coming as well'. Guiseppe draws eyes, nose and mouth: 'Hair, chin'. He runs inside and finds his name card 'Look "J" for Guiseppe that's me'. He makes marks for each letter. Guiseppe tells his friend, 'I made my aeroplane'. He then flies it around the garden.

Saja watches her peers playing with the water. She then selects a bottle and fills it with water and pours it into the Funky Fountain. When it comes out through the bungs she laughs. She refills her bottle with water and pours it into the fountain again. Saja quickly bends down and closes the bungs to stop the water coming out. She then opens them and tries to catch the water in a cup. Another child asks Saja if he could fill up her cup with the pump. Saja smiles and moves her cup next to the pump so it can be filled.

Olivia is in the role play area: 'The muffins are ready'. She puts on an oven glove and gets muffins out of the oven. Her friends come over and start to take them from the baking tray: 'No wait! They're hot'. 'I made pie for the baby, its banana pie. Here you go'. Olivia finds a spoon and pretends to feed the baby: 'I need a bib'. Her friend puts a bib on the baby and Olivia sits down and starts to feed the baby. When she gets up to get something her friend sits in the chair and continues feeding the baby. When Olivia comes back she asks, 'Can I sit there? Can I have a turn?'. Her friend doesn't want to move and Olivia says 'It's ok, we can do it together'. Olivia picks up a beaker and gives the baby a drink while her friend feeds the baby from the spoon.

These examples provide a vivid impression of the rich and varied learning that has been happening in the nursery every day of the year. It is interesting to see how every example relates to the characteristics of effective learning – these children have been learning effectively for the whole year. No wonder they have made such dramatic progress. As the year ends, the children are sad to be leaving nursery, but excited about their next step – into reception. They have a love of learning that has been nurtured and maintained by staff who are dedicated to working in a child-led style, trusting that the children will explore, learn and develop if they are given the right environment and support. The staff are leaving for a well-earned rest – ready to start the whole cycle again in September!

Conclusion

Visitors to Carterhatch nursery notice the confidence, independence and 'can do' attitude of our children that shines through in everything that they do. It is these attributes that will serve the children well as they carry on through our education system. They started nursery with a natural desire to learn and this has been exploited and enhanced – ensuring outstanding progress. The children have maintained their autonomy and unique identity – no two children have had the same experience of nursery and all feel that they have been in charge of their own learning. For those lucky enough to be staying at Carterhatch, this autonomy will continue into reception and therefore their love of learning will continue too!

So how has this been achieved?

The nursery is organised so that each child can decide where to go (indoors or outside), which resources to use, what to do with those resources, whether to be alone or with others, and for how long to pursue an activity. Thus they become deeply involved in their task, their brains are 'lit up' and progress is happening constantly. Their level of involvement might drop for a variety of reasons: they might not know how to do something, they might not be able to use a piece of equipment, another child might be disrupting them, they might need another resource, they might not have the language to communicate their ideas etc. When this happens the child will persevere for a while and will then seek help – either from another child or from an adult. This then becomes a teachable moment – a chance for a skilled adult to join the child, assess what is needed and then to give them the skill, knowledge, resource, vocabulary or advice that they need in order to carry on. Some such moments are recorded – on 'learning journeys', on 'planning in the moment sheets' and in Special Books.

This sounds quite straightforward but I hope that, if you have read this book, you will realise that the nursery is meticulously planned and organised, with clear and consistent boundaries, within which the children have the freedom to explore and learn, supported by skilled staff. When I try to explain what needs to be in place for truly child-led learning to be successful, it often reminds me of 'spinning plates' as the picture below indicates. You need the environment to be perfect **and** you need the highest quality of interactions (teaching) **and** you need enough highly trained staff **and** you need to keep accurate, meaningful and useful records and assessments **and** you need parents to work in partnership with you **and** you need to have clear boundaries and expectations.

While all the plates are spinning, progress will be outstanding. If any 'plate' falls, then the whole system can collapse: a poor environment means the children will not be involved (and therefore not learning); poor interactions (i.e. not teaching) mean that learning opportunities will be missed; not enough staff results in teachable moments being missed; meaningless paperwork (rather than appropriate and manageable paperwork) leads to less time for interactions (i.e. less teaching); parents not 'on board' will cause anxiety in the children (and prevent learning); and lack of boundaries and expectations can lead to disruption in the class (again preventing learning).

I have 25 years of experience in teaching and for many of those years I was not at all happy about the pedagogies that I was forced to follow. Since developing a system of child-initiated learning with 'planning in the moment', I feel totally confident that it is the best possible approach for the children. The outstanding progress that we achieve is testament to our success. We meet the needs, interests and stage of development of each unique child, by supporting them to pursue their own interests.

Children are born with a desire to learn – it is innate. It does not disappear when they enter a setting – be that a child-minder's, a preschool, a nursery or a reception class – they still want to learn. A setting, therefore, needs to exploit that desire by providing a superb environment, giving the children genuine choice and freedom, with skilled staff available to support and teach them when appropriate.

Unfortunately, in recent years there has been growing pressure to impose inappropriate and ineffective formal styles of teaching on our youngest children. There have been truly appalling examples of 'best practice' on the OFSTED website, as well as ill-informed and harmful messages from government ministers.

We, the practitioners, who work with our youngest children every day, know the truth. We know what is needed and what is appropriate. Thanks to the support and conviction of my head teacher, I have been able to put my pedagogy into practice – with the best possible outcomes for the children and the school.

The system I advocate in this book has been introduced in numerous settings up and down the country and in some international schools too. The results have been amazing as feedback from staff shows: 'We got the best ever feedback from OFSTED (team leader, Manchester); 'Our good level of development jumped by 20 per cent' (reception teacher, Kent); 'The class is much calmer because all the children are absorbed in what they are doing' (assistant head, Ilford); 'I know the children so well this year. This system has let me enjoy my job again' (nursery teacher, Enfield); 'My job is still hard work, but the work now benefits the children – and we have great fun too!' (reception teacher, London). The feedback from parents is equally persuasive: 'My son now loves to go to school. Today he went to bed early so he could get up early and get to school to carry on with his pirate ship!'; 'The most significant thing is my daughter's confidence in learning and trying to do things and not giving up'; 'This play-based system enhances learning. I love the way my daughter is free to make her own ideas and opinions, which has made her more confident'.

As the comments above clearly show – this is a win–win situation – best for the children, best for the staff and best for the setting. There is a saying 'If you always do what you have always done, you will always get what you have always got!'. If you want

something different for the staff and children, then try something new. The only way to know if this system works is to try it and see the results.

I have been coordinating teams to use this child-led system for eight years and I have seen the result – it allows the staff to love teaching and the children to love learning! Surely that is the best possible way to educate our children!

Appendix A: Ferre Laevers' levels of involvement

Involvement focuses on the extent to which pupils are operating to their full capabilities. In particular it refers to whether the child is focused, engaged and interested in various activities.

The Leuven Scale for Involvement specifies:

1 Low activity
   Activity at this level can be simple, stereotypic, repetitive and passive. The child is absent and displays no energy. There is an absence of cognitive demand. The child characteristically may stare into space. N.B. This may be a sign of inner concentration.

2 A frequently interrupted activity
   The child is engaged in an activity but half of the observed period includes moments of non-activity, in which the child is not concentrating and is staring into space. There may be frequent interruptions in the child's concentration, but his/her involvement is not enough to return to the activity.

3 Mainly continuous activity
   The child is busy at an activity but it is at a routine level and the real signals for involvement are missing. There is some progress but energy is lacking and concentration is at a routine level. The child can be easily distracted.

4 Continuous activity with intense moments
   The child's activity has intense moments during which activities at Level 3 can come to have special meaning. Level 4 is reserved for the kind of activity seen in those intense moments, and can be deduced from the 'involvement signals'. This level of activity is resumed after interruptions. Stimuli, from the surrounding environment, however attractive, cannot seduce the child away from the activity.

5 Sustained intense activity
   The child shows continuous and intense activity revealing the greatest involvement. In the observed period not all the signals for involvement need be there, but the essential ones must be present: concentration, creativity, energy and persistence. This intensity must be present for almost all the observation period.

Level of involvement

Time	Involvement	Comments
Average		

Appendix B: Learning journey 2014

Learning journey for .... Term .... Date ....

Entries should include the initial observation (and assessment), the teaching and the outcome.

P R I M E	COMMUNICATION AND LANGUAGE
	PHYSICAL DEVELOPMENT
	PERSONAL, SOCIAL AND EMOTIONAL DEVELOPMENT
S P E C I F I C	LITERACY
	MATHEMATICS
	UNDERSTANDING THE WORLD
	EXPRESSIVE ARTS AND DESIGN
	Obs indoors
	Obs outdoors
	Parent consultation

Identified areas for focus:

General/parents:

Profile:

*

*

*

Identified areas for future focus:

General/parents:

Profile:

*   *   *

Appendix C: Planning in the moment

Planning in the moment

	PRIME AREAS			SPECIFIC AREAS			
	C&L	PHD	PSE	LIT	MATHS	UW	EXP A&D
Areas covered:							

W/C: Term:

Focus children: *   *   *

                     *   *   *

Monday	Tuesday	Wednesday	Thursday	Friday

	Observation and Assessment	(Plan and) Teaching	Outcome (observation)
1			
2			
3			
4			
5			
6			

Photo Gallery:

Appendix D: Story scribing

- Sit beside the child (if you are right handed, put the child on your left).
- Make sure the child watches you write (i.e. the paper should be in front of the child if possible). Write exactly what the child says.
- Use your knowledge of each child to decide which teaching is appropriate.
- Say the words as you write them.
- Sometimes stop and read what you have written and then let the child carry on.
- Sound out some words as you write them.
- Point out spaces, capitals and full stops etc.
- Exaggerate some letter formation.
- Ask the child to sound out some words for you.
- Ask the child to write a few letters – or words – as appropriate to the individual child.
- Use terms such as 'characters', 'author' etc.
- The *story* is the important part – keep the momentum – the teaching should not slow down the scribing too much.

Anna Ephgrave

Appendix E: Playdough recipe

You will need:

1 cup of salt
2 cups of plain flour
2 tablespoons of cream of tartar
2 tablespoons of cooking oil
2 cups of boiling water
Food colouring
Large bowl

Mix all the ingredients in a large bowl.

If you keep the dough in a plastic bag or an airtight container, it will last about six weeks.

Appendix F: Cake recipe

You can use:

1 egg or
2 eggs or 3 eggs or
4 eggs or 5 eggs or 6 eggs
More eggs = bigger cake!

- 1 -

Balance the eggs
with the flour.

Put the flour
in the bowl

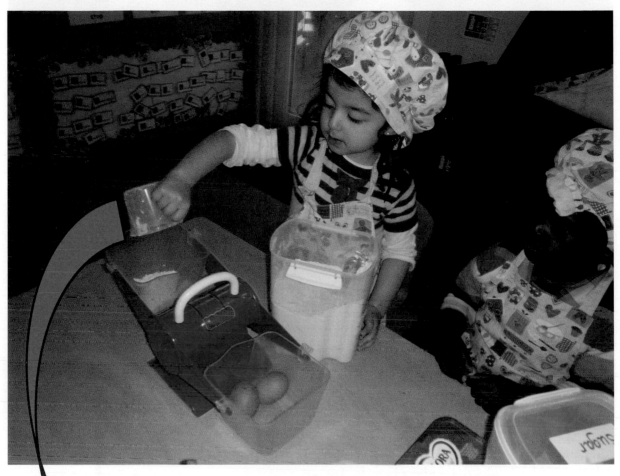

Balance the eggs
with the sugar.

Put the sugar
in the bowl.

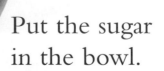

Balance the eggs
with the butter.

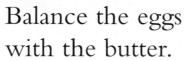

Put the butter
in the bowl.

– 4 –

Add the eggs
to the bowl.

Mix, mix, mix!

Put the mixture in a baking tray.

Cook at 180° C for 15 minutes.

Decorate your cake and eat it!

– 6 –

Appendix G: Suppliers list

Suppliers

www.creativecascade.co.uk – for Creative Cascade Sets, Welly Storage, Wood work benches and Funky Fountains (Products designed by Anna!)

Skips, ditches, parents (great suppliers of "junk modelling" resources), charity shops, etc.

DIY stores and online companies – for ropes, marine ply wood, pulleys, woodwork tools and elasticated rope.

www.communityplaythings.co.uk – for wooden blocks (various sizes) and storage units.

www.costco.co.uk – for heavy duty tarpaulins and shelving.

www.cosydirect.com – for open-ended resources at reasonable prices.

www.earlyexcellence.com – for open shelving in particular.

www.ikea.co.uk – for storage units, canopies and children's furniture.

www.impbins.com – for salt bins.

www.olympicgymnasium.com – for A-Frames and ladders etc. Look in their "nursery" section.

www.pvc-strip.co.uk – for plastic strips to hang in doorways.

www.shedstore.co.uk – for sheds (model: Larchlap Overlap Maxi Wallstore 63 is useful for storing large wooden blocks).

Consultancy/training

www.freedomtolearn.co.uk offer consultancy services with Anna Ephgrave and Ruth Moore, based on the methods described in this book as well as "environment make-over" work.

Bibliography

Athey, C. (1990) *Extending Thought in Young Children; A Parent–Teacher Partnership*. London: Paul Chapman Publishing Ltd.

Bilton, H. (2010) *Outdoor Learning in the Early Years*. Oxford: Routledge.

Bowlby, J. (1997) *Attachment and Loss*. London: Pimlico.

Brooker, L. (2002) *Starting School*. Oxford: Oxford University Press.

Bruce, T. (1987) *Early Childhood Education*. 3rd Edition 2005. London: Hodder and Stoughton.

Bruce, T. (2001) *Learning Through Play: Babies, Toddlers and the Foundation Years*. London: Hodder Arnold.

Department for Children, Schools and Families (2009) *Learning, Playing and Interacting*. National Strategies. London: Department for Children, Schools and Families.

DfES (Department for Education) (2007) *Early Years Foundation Stage*. Nottingham: DfES Publications.

DfES (Department for Education) (2014) *Early Years Foundation Stage*. Nottingham: DfES Publications.

Dyer, W. (2007) *Mercury's Child*. Booklocker.com, Inc. for Colly and Sons, UK.

Early Education (2012) Development Matters in the Early Years Foundation Stage (EYFS). Early Education, London www.foundationyears.org.uk/files/2012/03/Development-Matters-FINAL-PRINT-AMENDED.pdf

Ephgrave, A. (2012) *The Reception Year in Action*. 2nd Edition. Oxford: Routledge.

Fisher, J. (2002) *Starting From the Child*. 2nd Edition. Maidenhead: Open University Press.

Gerhardt, S. (2004) *Why Love Matters*. Hove: Routledge.

Gussin-Paley, V. (1991) *The Boy Who Would Be A Helicopter*. Cambridge, MA: Harvard University Press.

Isaacs, S. (1929) *The Nursery Years*. London: Routledge & Kegan Paul.

Isaacs, S. (1966) *Intellectual Growth in Young Children*. New York: Shockern Books.

Laevers, F. (1994) *Five Levels of Well-Being*. Leuven: Leuven University Press.

Legerstee, M., Haley, D. and Bornstein, M. (2013) *The Infant Mind*. New York: The Guilford Press.

Nutbrown, C. (2006) *Threads of Thinking*. 3rd Edition. London: Sage.

OFSTED (Office for Standards in Education, Children's Services and Skills) (2014) *Evaluation Schedule for Inspections of Registered Early Years Provision: Guidance and grade descriptors for inspecting registered early years provision*. London: OFSTED.

POST (Parliamentary Office of Science and Technology) (2000) *POST Report 140, Early Years Learning*. POST www.parliament.uk/post/pn140.pdf

Read, V. and Hughes, A. (2009) *Developing Attachment in Early Years Settings*. Oxford: David Fulton Publishers.

Robinson, D. and Groves, J. (2002) *Introducing Bertrand Russell*. Cambridge: Icon Books.

Russell, D. (1932) *In Defence of Children*. London: Hamish Hamilton.

Sylva, K., Melhuish, E.C., Sammons, P., Siraj-Blatchford, I. and Taggart, B. (2004) *The Effective Provision of Pre-School Education (EPPE) Project: Technical Paper 12 – The Final Report: Effective Pre-School Education*. London: DfES/Institute of Education, University of London.

Vygotsky, L.S. (1987) *Mind in Society*. Cambridge, MA: Harvard University Press.

Whalley, M. (20070 *Involving Parents in their Children's Learning*. 2nd Edition. London: Paul Chapman Publishing.

Index